Door Supervision

The Low Profile Skills

By Ronnie Gamble

All Rights Reserved

No part of this book may be reproduced in any form or by any means (photocopying or by any electronic or mechanical means, including information storage or retrieval systems) without permission in writing from both the copyright owner and the publisher of this book.

Ronnie Gamble has asserted the moral right to be identified as the author of this work.

Gamble © 2008

Warning

The techniques presented in work are for public information, entertainment and research purposes only.

This book is presented, subject to the following condition.

The author will not be held responsible for the psychological, physiological or material results of the application of any techniques described and illustrated in this work.

This work focuses on the Low Profile Skills and will not cover;

The Physical Skills
The Legal Limitations of Door Work
Emergency Evacuation
Basic Fire Fighting
Emergency First Aid
Civil and Criminal Law
Health and Safety at Work
Licensing Law

ISBN 978-1-4092-6619-8

Acknowledgements

I am indebted to Graham Mulholland for his proofreading, feedback, and additions and also Diana Kirkpatrick and my daughter Rhonda Gamble. They all went to great pains to sort out my dreadful use of the English language.

I would also like to thank Ben Ross and Chris Lowe for their feedback and corrections during the production of this work.

And to all the incompetent and abusive people I encountered on the door. That includes the bar managers, security managers, bar staff, off duty bar and door staff and finally the small circle of abusive customers. They all gave me an insight into that dark and depressing side of working the door.

And finally, to the other people I encountered who were in the majority, the customers, managers and staff who were a joy to work with. Without all of these diverse groups under my scrutiny I would have had little to write about.

By the same author

The Coleraine Battery: The History of 6 Light Anti-Aircraft Battery RA (SR) 1939-1945, Causeway Museum Service, Coleraine, 2006

Echo Company: The History of E Company 5th Battalion of the Ulster Defence Regiment, Regimental Association of the Ulster Defence Regiment, Coleraine Branch, Coleraine, 2007

My Service Life (1939-1979): William 'Bill' Balmer, Causeway Museum Service, Coleraine, 2009 (in production)

Contents

Acknowledgements		3
By the same author		4
Preface		6
Chapter 1	The Low Profile Skills	9
Chapter 2	The Security World	17
Chapter 3	Door Supervisor Profiles	31
Chapter 4	Basic Duties	43
Chapter 5	Searching	69
Chapter 6	Drug Awareness	77
Chapter 7	Intermediate Skills	87
Chapter 8	People Profiles	105
Chapter 9	Verbal Conflict Management	123
Chapter 10	Stress, Fear and Violence	135
Chapter 11	Tips and Tricks	151
Chapter 12	Non-Violent Incident Response Drills	169
Chapter 13	The Drunken Customer	185
Bibliography		195

Preface

The purpose of this work is to present the tactics I used during my time as a door supervisor and also explain my concept of the Low Profile Skills.

Much of this material was updated at 2 o'clock in the morning after an arduous session on the door. The strong language I sometimes had to use and also experienced every night is reflected in this work.

The theoretical material used in this book as well as the concept of the low profile skills have been derived from the psychology and behaviour modification research projects I conducted during my readings for a B.Sc. Honours degree in Social Psychology and Sociology.

The practical material in this book has been derived from my experiences as a head door supervisor as well as the training notes and observations I made while training door supervisors.

The training and operating procedures for door supervisors are going through a dynamic phase and the procedures set out in this work may conflict with the current training, culture and legislation in any particular country. This work must be read from that perspective.

A further book is in preparation and focuses on the physical skills I found to be the most successful when my encounters went beyond the verbal.

Door Supervising

The Low Profile Skills

Chapter 1

The Low Profile Skills

Door supervisors are primarily tasked with maintaining the security, the safety and the good order at any venue at which they are employed. That includes looking after all the customers, all the staff and the property at their venue.

But there are limits to the degree of good order that any door supervisor can maintain. Some of these limits are created by environmental and social influences that remain outside the control of door supervisors. In these situations, door supervisors will inevitably find themselves responding to problems rather than controlling their venue. I will outline these environmental and social influences in this chapter, expand on them throughout this work and also offer my coping strategies.

The Low Profile Skills

Some of the key skills I applied in my time 'on the door' were modified from the psychology and behaviour modification research projects I conducted during my readings for a B.Sc. Honours degree in Social Psychology and Sociology. I have labelled these, the 'Low Profile Skills'.

Low profile skills are the subtle physical and verbal techniques used by experienced door supervisors as they interact with and maintain the welfare and security of customers at their venues. These techniques include assertiveness, personal presentation, observation, psychological manipulation, physical manipulation, listening skills, body language, verbal conflict management, flexible and assertive negotiation, assertive arbitration, fear management, stress control and social interaction.

The low profile skills form a small part of the large repertoire of skills expected of the professional door supervisor. But in the general day-to-day running of venue security, the door supervisors who have developed their low profile skills will be able to reduce and manage the number of problems they have to deal with.

The Main Social and Environmental Influences

I have identified five main social interactions and environmental factors that influence customer and staff behaviour at licensed premises.

1. *The Venue Influence.* The structure, layout and management of the venue can create either positive or negative behaviours

2. *Learned Behaviour.* Customers and staff bring their social and cultural experiences to the venue

3. *Customer Interaction.* This takes place within and between all the different social groups at the venue

4. *Staff Interaction.* This takes place within and between the bar and door staff groups

5. *General Interaction.* This takes place between all those at the venue, the customers, the bar staff and the door staff

Diagram 1: The Influences on Customer Behaviour

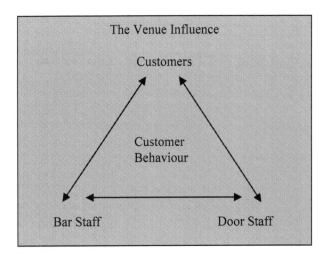

This diagram represents how customer behaviour is dependent on these five factors. Everyone brings learned behaviour to the venue but the venue environment overshadows and influences each individual. And

finally, not only do the customers, the bar staff and the door staff interact *within* their three groups; interaction also takes place *between* these three main groups. These five influences will encourage specific customer behaviour.

What Are The Specific Factors That Influence Behaviour?

In the next two tables I have listed in more detail elements from the first two factors, the venue influence and learned behaviour. These tables are based not only on my experiences as a door supervisor. They are also based on my interpretation of the sociological and psychological studies of the causal elements for customer behaviour on licensed premises.
Some of the elements appear to have been shoehorned into two categories just to make the presentation easy. For example, putting Stag and Hen parties in the low risk category on Table 2. But just because these groups force the bar and door staff to work hard it's not in itself a good enough excuse to exclude these groups. The risk they pose is usually low and I have made a point throughout this study of not mistaking hard work for high risk.

Table 1 contains many of the causal elements located in the venue that influence the behaviour of customers and staff. These are listed in the left hand column. The next two columns of this table show the high and low risk levels or indicators to expected behaviour.

Table 2 contains the causal elements that customers and staff bring to the venue. Again, these causal elements are listed in the left hand column of the table with the high and low risk indicators in the next two columns. If an individual displays the high-risk elements from this table, they must not gain entry to your venue.

Alcohol and Dysfunctional Behaviour

The tables also show that alcohol may be only one of the causal elements responsible for violence and dysfunctional behaviour at licensed premises. There are other causal elements to consider for that behaviour.
That may be a difficult concept to accept but many studies claim to show that it is a cluster of elements coming together at licensed premises that leads to a higher risk of violence or dysfunctional behaviour. I will use the remainder of this work to explain in more detail the elements listed on the following two tables.

Table 1: How the Venue Influences the Customers and Staff

Subject	High Risk	Low Risk
Alcohol	Aggressive Promotion Fixed Measures Low Pricing Happy Hours Slow Service Irresponsible Serving	Alternatives to Alcohol Choice of Measures Food Served Higher Prices Quick Service Responsible Serving
Environment	Crowded Noisy Dark Hot Dirty Bar Dirty Toilets No Glass Collection Poor Decoration Trouble Spots No Family Areas	Crowd Control Relaxed Good Lighting Comfortable Clean Bar Clean Toilets Glass Collectors Well Decorated Revised Layouts Family Catering
Security	Poor Observation No Cameras No Radios No Incident Response Drills Poor Reputation Bottles and Glasses	Good Observation Well Placed CCTV Adequate Communication Incident Response Drills Fair Reputation More Plastic
Bar & Security Staff	Incompetent Management Low Numbers Poorly Trained Argumentative Aggressive Uncaring Aloof Scruffy Inarticulate Non Responsive No Customer Monitoring	Sound Management Up to Strength Skilled Assertive Polite Caring Approachable Well Dressed Articulate Pro Active & Pre Emptive Customer Monitoring
Time	Weekend 10 pm.-2 am	Mid Week Mid Day

Table 2: How the Customers and Staff Influence the Venue

Subject	High Risk	Low Risk
Alcohol & Drugs	Taken Hidden	Sober
Weapons	Hidden	None
Personality Type	Psychotic Introvert Unstable Psychopath	Extrovert Gregarious
Appearance	Scruffy Work Clothes Street Clothes Gang Colours	Clean Tidy Best Dress
Reputation	Previously Cautioned Criminal	Well Behaved Caring
Mood & Attitude	Angry Sad Tense Arrogant	Happy Calm Relaxed
Social Origins	High Deprivation Abusive Family	Crime Free Caring Family
Cultural Expectation	Cultural Groupings Street Drinking Habits	All Same Culture Disciplined Home Life
Social Skills	Inarticulate Submissive Aggressive Under Age Habituation	Articulate Assertive
Social Grouping	Young Males Gangs Rival Team Supporters Strangers	Mixed Genders Mixed Age Group Stag & Hen Parties Young Families

Verbal Conflict Management

Verbal conflict can be a precursor to physical conflict. That fact alone makes learning how to manage verbal conflict situations an essential skill.

The Three Stages

The management of verbal conflict has three stages,

1. Categorizing the Verbal Conflict

2. Selecting the Response

3. Reinforcing the Response

The door supervisor has to categorize and then manage at least three types of verbal conflict. These categories are,

1. Complaining customers

2. Rule breakers

3. Customers who are arguing between themselves

Once the verbal conflict has been categorised it becomes much easier to select the ideal response and then reinforce that response.
Complaining customers and rule breakers demand a personal response and customers who are arguing between themselves demand an intrusive response.

This concept of verbal conflict management is set out in the following diagram. Good and bad examples of negotiation and arbitration are provided throughout this work. Chapter 9 will deal in more depth with this terminology and the stages of verbal conflict management.

Diagram 2: Verbal Conflict Management

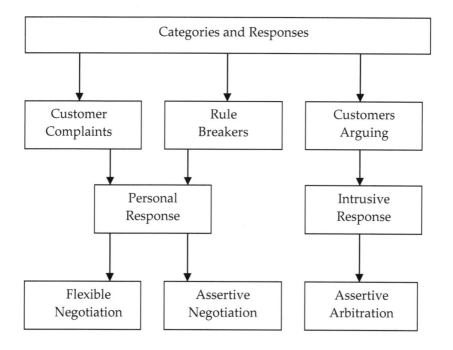

Chapter 2

The Security World

Stewards and door supervisors are expected to manage, cater and care for the customers at their event. These tasks place a high demand on the individual's social interaction and communication skills.

Door supervisors can be employed as stewards. The latter however, are not usually employed as door supervisors. This is because door supervisors have an edge on stewards, and it is this: door supervisors must have a proven track record for coping with both verbal aggression and physical violence. Not only must they be capable of detecting a potentially aggressive situation they must also be capable of pre-empting and defusing it. Not everybody has both the physical skill and the moral courage to carry out this onerous task.

Where Are Door Supervisors Employed?

It is the responsibility of event organisers to provide a safe environment for all customers, artistes and staff, as far as reasonably practicable. Event organisers have to eliminate the risk of accidents and disasters. Every planned event must have crowd management procedures based on the event organiser's risk assessment of that event. Therefore, there will always be a demand for the multi-skilled professional door supervisors.

Properly trained and qualified door supervisors are in great demand at indoor or outdoor venues where people have to be managed and stewarded. That includes Race Meetings, Soccer Matches, Rugby Matches, Firework Displays, Rock Concerts, Pop Festivals, Dirt Track Events and Government Committee meetings open to the public.

The mere presence of door supervisors, whatever their ability, will help to deter theft, assault, property damage and other illegal activity at any venue. But, other than the mere deterrent value, the task now demands many professional qualities.

A Day at the Races

The low profile skills have their own part to play in managing these events. But each of these events has a unique set of safety, security and crowd management problems. These problems are beyond the scope of the stereotypical or traditional door supervisor.

Bikers Are Good Guys Where I Come From

How Dangerous is Door Work?

Compared to other occupations, door work is relatively safe when you operate in a professional manner. The National Institute of Occupational Safety and Health (USA, 1995), who have their website at, http://www.cdc.gov/niosh/homicide.html shows that homicide accounts for twelve percent of all deaths in the workplace. Top of the death list is the taxicab service followed by liquor store operatives and then filling station operatives. Security work is fourth in line. What the first three occupations have in common is the following,

- The victims are usually working alone

- The victims are responsible for handling cash

- The victims work late into the small hours of the morning

The Physical Injuries to Expect

The most common physical injuries you can experience will include cracked ribs, lost teeth, bouncers eye, bloody nose, black eyes, busted lips, broken tail bones and bursitis of the knees and elbows from ground fighting on the street, strained back from the sudden physical demands, bitten fingers and thumbs, minor scratches and finally, a bruised skull from collecting drunken bum punches on the top of the head.
There will be nights when the door staff will find themselves standing and praying that it will be a quiet night as they are suffering from some of these minor injuries.

The Physical Demands on Door Supervisors

On a good quiet night the physical demands on door supervisors will be minimal. But when a physical confrontation takes place the physical demands are severe. If the confrontation becomes a protracted operation, for whatever reason, the adrenalin rush will drain your strength reserves. Under these circumstances you are more likely to strike out or make a mistake.
The physical demands will be reduced if you develop your social interaction skills and learn to maintain a genuine attitude of care for the customers.

Why Should You Become a Door Supervisor?

- Many door supervisors enjoy meeting and watching different artistes and personalities

- Many door supervisors prefer social interaction as opposed to vegetating in front of the TV

- Some individuals use their wages to finance a hobby, yearly holidays or pay off their debts

- Other door supervisors enjoy meeting people from diverse cultures, races, creeds and interests

- There are opportunities to be at the front line in news worthy or politically significant events

- There is immense job satisfaction in being capable of managing and controlling dangerous situations

- If someone has a dull 9-5 routine, then working two nights a week on the doors will give them a buzz

- 'Doing the Door' is a first class remedy for constipation

Forget About Becoming a Door Supervisor

- The public have a stereotypical view of door supervisors as thugs in Tuxedos.

- The public is acquainted with the legal limitations on door supervisors and the more socially challenged customers will use this information to abuse door supervisors

- The wages for the average door supervisors are at or below legal minimum levels

- Door supervisors' work is totally unsocial. While customers are 'winding down' the door supervisors are definitely 'winding up'

- If you are doing the job properly, you will go home both physically and emotionally exhausted

- The job is dangerous, screw up any risk assessment and your life is on the line

- Try pre-emptive strikes with a security camera on you. Your justification and the prosecutor's interpretation of the event are always diametrically opposed

- Minimum force rules and self-defence rules are stood on their head. You have to face the problem without running away

- You have to learn to cope with the long term anxiety, stress and the constant recall of abusive incidents

Six of The Best Reasons For Moving On

1. When you feel like it

2. When you do not have the support of the bar manager or security manager for your actions or decisions

3. When you find out your 'Back Up' has a family, drink or drug problem or no balls

4. When your employer has no form of insurance that covers your medical or legal fees

5. When you have not been updated in your door supervisor skills by an accredited training team

6. When drug dealers, thugs or paramilitaries take over your area

The Emotional Demands on Door Supervisors

The most serious drain on your system is the emotional demand. This includes the anxiety experienced long before you reach the venue. On some nights you can be left short handed because an individual 'caved in' to this experience.

At times the job of door supervisor can be viewed as thankless. Customers are enjoying themselves and 'winding down.' You are not enjoying yourself and definitely 'winding up.'
As a door supervisor, there will be no shortages in 'wind up merchants' or situations to upset your emotional stability.

- Bar staff may continually break the house rules and security precautions, leaving you to cope with irate bar managers

- Customers will drink too much and use this as an excuse to infringe house rules or threaten you

- Customers who question your abilities, age, experience and qualifications

- Bar managers may infringe Health and Safety, Disability Legislation and Drink Laws, leaving you to cope with it

- You screw up on the door in that someone bluffs his or her way into the venue and the rest of the team have to sort it out

- You are always failing to stay one jump ahead of the bar manager and your head supervisor

When you lose your emotional stability, this will compound your problems. At times, it may prove difficult to control your emotions.
By remaining impersonal, assertive and non-argumentative, it is possible to maintain a professional cool.

The emotional roller coaster of a demanding night will always leave you emotionally high. You will probably spend over an hour unwinding after the duty is finished.

A Day In The Life of a Door Supervisor

An average day would produce very little to write up. For me, the following type of day comes every fourth day on the job.

8 - 5:00 pm   A normal day's work at your full time employment.

5:30 pm   A phone call from the security firm, telling you to be at The XXXXX Bar from 7:30 pm until midnight. Within ten minutes you have this massive urge for a crap. That is the effect that some rough jobs have on your constitution.

7:15 pm   Meet up at the bar with your partner for the night. You can smell the vomit on his breath.

7:30 pm   Clear the bar of drunks, barred individuals and under-age drinkers.

7:45 pm   Your anxiety levels start to drop as you make your mark and start to work the crowd. As the evening goes on you continually talk to your partner about potential problems, people to watch and others that require talking to.

8:00 pm   Your partner is approached by one of the bar staff. They have pointed out someone who is drunk and causing trouble. Your partner approaches the individual and asks him to leave the bar, as he appears to be too drunk. This individual was in reality just talking to his friends, who now tell your partner to back off, as they will look after him.

Your partner has backed off, but you can see he has started to 'lose the plot'. He is now standing rigid and staring at the group and you know that if one of them accidentally farts loudly he is going to rip their head off. The group also note this and within ten minutes they approach him, shake hands and apologize. They also call a cab for their friend, and the situation is resolved.

As a door supervisor, you must always take a couple of seconds to carry out a risk assessment before committing yourself. Sometimes acting immediately on either false or misleading information will set you up for a losing situation.

9:00 pm   The crowd is now 380 strong. You feel easy because there is a good mix of male and female within each group. The average age within each group is in the 20's, so you feel confident about working this mature, well-dressed and stable crowd.

10:00 pm   The crowd drops to 280, but the bar staff has a difficulty in coping with them and are considering closing the doors.

This is because; the crowd at 9:00 pm were relatively sober. Despite the drop from 380 to 280, that extra hour's drinking time gives you a much noisier and more abusive crowd.

Once you work at a bar for at least one month, and filtered all the under age drinkers, scum and street trash from the regular customers, you can virtually predict the general behaviour and noise levels of the crowd. The younger, and the more immature the crowd is, the quicker they will drink. This leads to a rapid loss of inhibitions and therefore more trouble. The noise levels peak much earlier with a younger crowd of customers. But, if you have removed all the rubbish, this noise level will not be as threatening to both you and other bar staff. In the bad old days, before you weeded the place out, this noise level was always a precursor to serious trouble.

11:00 pm   The crowd drops to 150 as everyone leaves for the local nightclubs after tanking up on cheap booze. You are now left with the hard core of serious drinkers.

11:15 pm   Last orders are called.

11:30 pm   You now have 30 minutes to clear the bar of the heavy drinkers.

11:35 pm   Despite all your efforts to work the crowd and pre-empt problems, it goes ballistic on you. The bar staff draw your attention to the far end of the bar. At one of the quietest tables, a customer has decided to smash a bottle across the forehead of his best friend and now there is blood flying in every direction.

By the time you reach the incident, the victim is getting help from his friends to staunch the flow of blood and the offender is still standing in a rage. Your partner starts to lead the offender to the door and you cover his back. He slips on the broken bottles and the offender seizes the opportunity to start an attack on him, you nail him to the wall with a horizontal elbow strike to the side of the neck below his ear, which cools him down.

At this stage his friend turns up and promises to escort him off the premises. When he reaches the door, the offender states he has left his mobile phone at the table. Your partner scuttles off to retrieve the item. The offender then starts pumping up on adrenaline again and decides to take you on. Despite being held back by a much heavier friend, they both pile into you. You go down below them.

You give the offender a bad day again by clamping your thumbs in below the ears at the jaw hinges, squeezing like mad and straightening out your arms. The offender is definitely having a bad day, so you lift your left foot and plant it near your right knee, pushing off and turning clockwise. This gives you the upper position. You break your legs free from the tangle of legs and the offender's friend takes the subdued individual off the premises.

When things go ballistic, you must operate with back up to reduce the personal threat. Fright leads to freeze, fight, flight or inappropriate behaviour. On this occasion my back up decided to retrieve a mobile phone to escape from the hostile zone.

Sometimes, despite all your training and experience, you simply screw up. If you take your eyes off a troublemaker as he pumps up his adrenalin you will get hit. During the quiet periods of my life, I can remember most of my fights in great detail and even muse about the alternative openings I could have capitalised on.

This fracas bugged me because the preceding fraction of a second before the pile up always came back to me as a blank spot in my memory of the incident. On this occasion, I had decided not to hit the offender because he was being held by his friend... bad mistake. I was caught out because I was using the wrong mind set for a violent situation. Always, even when the opposition is under restraint, maintain 'The Edge' by staying prepared to strike.

Using a defensive, passive or neutral mind set in a violent situation will get you killed. Always maintain an instrumental violence mind set, this will give you 'The Edge' in any situation. I define instrumental violence as the use of controlled and reasonable force to achieve an objective.

This will be covered in more detail in the next book 'Door Supervising: The Physical Skills'.

11:40 pm   Offender and friend leave.

11:45 pm   Police arrive but the victim refuses to make a statement. The police then leave.

Midnight   The bar has been cleared and the staff are cleaning up. We complete the incident book.

12:30 am   Home; steeping blood stains out of the shirt and trying to wind down.

1:00 am   Bed. Staring at the ceiling again.

2:00 am   Asleep

A Year in the Life of a Door Supervisor

The following table shows the number of incidents that door staff responded to over the period of one year. These incidents occurred at the weekends when the venue was covered, eventually, by three door supervisors. The average number of customers each night was 180. This varied from 420 at the start of the year to 150 per night at the end of the year.
The reductions in the number of customers and a massive reduction in serious incidents were achieved by applying the preventive measures to be discussed later.

Table 3: A Year of Incidents Summary

Type Of Incident	How Often
Arguments Stopped	23
Door Supervisors Attacked + Fights Stopped	45
Mob Attack on Door Supervisors	2
Free For All Fights	3
Door Supervisors Threatened + Insulted	Every Night
Barring Individuals For Serious House Rule Infringements	50
Drunks and Others Ejected	95
Under Age Drinkers or No ID Refused Entry	147
Drunks/Barred and the Improperly Dressed Refused Entry	70
Bar Damage Incidents	7
Closed The Doors For Overcrowding and Fights at the Door	5
Reported Health and Safety Problems to the Bar Manager	12

A Quick Reality Check

The following report is a true story of all that can and will go wrong for door supervisors. It sets out in detail the failure of a bar manager to carry out his duties in a professional manner and the failure of the security company to support their door staff. The end result was the resignation of all the door staff and the resignation of the bar manager.
Despite the high standards in behaviour and professionalism expected from door staff, those same high standards are not exercised enough by their employers, the bar and security managers.
On some occasions over the past forty years I found that the employers of door staff did behave as though they are only qualified in maintaining their high profits and exploiting their door staff.

To. XXXX Security

Report on the Door Security Staffing Problems at XXXX Bar

The supply of regular door staff at XXXX has reached a crisis point for three main reasons.

1. The first reason concerns the bar managers incompetence.

2. The second reason concerns the rates of pay for door staff at XXXX Bar, as they are too low.

3. The third reason concerns XXXXX Security who have failed to react positively to this information.

Points of Contention

Manning Requirements. At present, Saturday nights have proved to be very popular with the customers. Last year the peak figures on a Saturday night were 120-180. This year the attendance has started to peak at 350 and 400.

There are only two door staff employed to cover three doors and two floors. This staffing level and customer care provision is criminally inadequate. Instead of being proactive and pre-emptive, the door staff are reduced to scurrying about from crisis to crisis.

Seating Capacity. In the past four years, the bar managers have never answered this question, "What is the seating capacity of this bar?"

Harassment. On many occasions duty bar managers will order door staff to throw out a customer for a minor misdemeanour without assessing either the risk to or the door staff priorities. Within two minutes the duty bar manager will approach the door staff again and enquire as to why the guy is still on the premises.

Radio Maintenance. After the weekend, the bar manager has five days to service and charge the radio batteries. This is not happening and the door staff are continually caught out without a working radio.

Managerial Bias. When questioned about a decision that went against the door staff, the bar manager stipulated that he would always accept the word of and support his bar staff at all times. He continues to maintain and exercise this bias.

Weak Leadership. It has always been impossible for the bar manager to adequately resolve security problems or problems between door staff, bar staff and off duty bar staff. This is possible with other junior bar managers but with the bar manager your approach was always stonewalled, a waste of time.

The bar manager continues to make security changes without informing the door staff.

The bar manager also freezes in the face of more serious problems. For example, on one occasion he ignored the two door staff standing at the door bleeding for three hours after a messy extraction.

The bar manager has tried to compromise the integrity of the door staff by engineering entrapment situations. For example, door staff have been left alone in the manager's office for 10 minutes surrounded by the daily takings. The computer monitor that displayed the view from the office camera was switched off.

Pay. At £6 an hour, the rate of pay for the door staff at XXXX Bar is below the local area levels. This is set at £7.50. Most of the door staff who leave XXXX Bar do so to move to higher paid venues.

Summary. Other than low wages, the current crisis is not the result of deterioration in the working relationship between any of the door or bar staff. The current crisis was caused by the bar manager's general incompetence and specific bias towards the door staff and your failure to react positively to this information.

The door staff have always left because they no longer wanted to be victims of situations created by the bias and weak leadership of the bar manager. In the past XXXX Bar have employed good bar managers, hopefully....

There are only two door staff left on the duty rota with little prospect of those who have left of ever returning.

Chapter 3

Door Supervisor Profiles

This chapter discusses the negative stereotyping of door supervisors and the psychological profile of the ideal door supervisor.

Negative Stereotyping of the Door Supervisor

Despite meeting all the basic requirements in dress, appearance, and social skills, the door supervisor often has to cope with negative stereotyping by the public.

The negative stereotyping of door supervisors is a process whereby an individual places all door supervisors in the same negative category. They associate any violence with the door supervisor, always assuming that the door supervisor initiated the incident. This process is also termed the self-fulfilling prophecy. The door supervisor can work well all night but as soon as it all goes wrong, it was his fault because that's his nature.

On one occasion, I experienced this negativity. As I waved my hand in front of a potential troublemaker and told him to move off, he bit my thumb. While I was standing moaning and groaning and my partner was trying to extract my thumb from the manic mouth clamp of a little toe-rag, two individuals approached, shouting, "Leave the poor boy alone, you bastards!"

The Source of the Negative Stereotyping

This negative stereotyping of door supervisors is not only based on the false perceptions of the public. The venue environment is also responsible for creating negative stereotypes, including;

- The Door Supervisor's Appearance

- The Perceived Danger

- The Door Supervisor's Role

- The Outsiders

- Blaming the Victim

The Door Supervisor's Appearance   Door supervisors are usually expected to dress uniformly in black. It has been noted athletes dressed in black not only viewed themselves, but others also viewed them as being more aggressive (Frank & Gilovich 1988).
To counter this problem, it might be better if the 'men in black' disappeared from the door and a different uniform and colour was introduced for all door and floor staff.

The Perceived Danger   Leather and Lawrence (1995) have found out that a venue employing door staff created a negative influence for that venue. Customers perceived the atmosphere in such bars to be more tense and less than friendly. To counter this problem, the customer must be made aware of the changed role of the door supervisor and floorwalker.

The Door Supervisor's Roles   The behaviour of one group of door supervisors can negatively influence the attitude of customers towards all door supervisors. This is particularly true when the customer is not aware of the correct role of the door supervisor. For example, in some bars the door supervisors gain a bad reputation because they always go in heavy handed when they respond to a problem.
In other bars, the door supervisors may be considered useless because of their soft, humanitarian or liberal approach to problems at their venue. This is where the door supervisors use the procedure of warning off unruly customers before ejecting them. Some customers may walk out of the venue, complaining about the unruly conduct of other customers.
Today, the unruly customers are given a chance to mend their ways before they are finally asked to leave the venue. The days of thump and dump are long gone. In these two examples, the door supervisors have created negative attitudes in customers. In the first example, acting

incorrectly created the negative attitude. In the second incident acting correctly created the negative attitude.

The Outsiders   Door supervisors can be treated as an out-group. This is because their behaviour and life style is different to the general population. The population is relaxing and unwinding after a days work but the door supervisors finish their normal work and then go on to control the doors. Because of this difference, they become an isolated and vulnerable group.

While carrying out their duties, door supervisors are always being verbally and physically abused by the frustrated, drunk and evil people in society. The real source of an individual's frustration may not be available or else may be too powerful to address directly. Because of this set of circumstances, the drunk or frustrated person attacks the door supervisor.

Blaming the Victim   The Social Role Theory of LeVine and Campbell 1972 (in Brewer & Crano, 1994) helps to explain the negative labelling of door supervisors. The behaviour, role and characteristics of the door supervisor's work, in having to respond to and also be a victim of abuse, are sometimes seen as the dispositions and characteristics of the door supervisors themselves.

This association with verbal and physical abuse is responsible for causing the formation of hostile attitudes towards door supervisors. The end product of this convoluted thinking process is that all door supervisors become labelled as abusive people.

Perhaps town councillors and leaders of the night time economy will give more public prominence to the training requirements, the standards expected and courses undertaken by door supervisors. This can be achieved by using the resources of the local media on a regular basis.

What Type of Person Becomes a Door Supervisor?

The ideal door supervisor must be mentally stable, reliable and honest. They must have highly developed social skills and be able to think fast and move fast when presented with any form of problem.

There are many other qualities an employer or head door supervisor expects. But these qualities can only be reciprocated if the door supervisors are treated in the same courteous and caring manner they are expected to exercise on customers and bar staff.

Generally speaking most door supervisors I have worked with were from the skilled working classes. They proved to be a hard core of dependable individuals who had an insignificant number of financial problems, drug and drink dependence, sexual hang-ups, fetishes, religious quirks, political leanings, gender prejudices, disability phobias or other personality defects. They were all able to interact positively with all the customers they met and bid farewell to.

The selection of an individual as a door supervisor is an ongoing process. After the initial security screening, profiling, training and tick tests there is another selection process. That one takes place on the job and it is designed to weed out the last of the rubbish, the psychopaths, cowards, liars, drug dealers, bullies and the useless that all managed to get through the early process.

Professional door supervisors must be constantly security screened, trained and tested so that they are up to date with the current trends and legislation. This procedure protects the customers in their care and the door staff themselves.

Psychological Factors that Effect the Behaviour of Door Supervisors

There are three main psychological factors that affect the behaviour of door supervisors. These factors are,

1. Attitude

2. Personality Type

3. Moral Courage

Attitude

An attitude is a mind set, a collection of beliefs as well as an orientation towards a specific subject. Experience helps to mould our attitudes and these attitudes can be altered by new experiences, such as a training programme. Attitude has a direct affect on the behaviour of a door supervisor. If their attitude towards the job and their practical ability is strongly interrelated, you will see a good door supervisor in action.

If a door supervisor has the attitude that he wants to do a good job on the door, but lacks the knowledge and practical ability to perform that task, then his performance will not mirror his intent.

In this section there are four examples of attitude. The first pair will be negative and the last pair will be positive.

The Neanderthal The first example of poor attitude concerns the yesterday men of door supervisor work. I am describing 'The Neanderthal', who sometimes appears on TV or radio interviews and will force you to cringe behind the potato couch in embarrassment. This type of person is also the wife beater, the bully, the murderer and the psychopath.

The Neanderthals are well known for their hostile attitudes towards all customers. Their sole purpose in life is to do unto some little toe rag what parents or the police had failed to do. The Neanderthal will sort out and chastise any little bugger that dares to step out of line. Rather than guide or steer young people who are away from their family environment, the Neanderthal operates to his own banal agenda by intimidating and abusing those in his care.

The Naïve The second example of poor attitude is the naïve young door supervisor. These individuals try to be polite to everybody, hoping that behaviour will be returned Fat chance.
This type of door supervisor has probably finished the Door Supervisors Registration course with top marks on the tick test. He will soon learn that this classroom knowledge has done nothing to help him to interact with others in the real world.
His attitude, focused on doing a good job on the door, will not be reflected in his behaviour because he lacks the practical experience.

Crocodile Dundee The first example of the correct attitude to be displayed by door supervisors is that of the competent controllers. They are experienced door supervisors who understand the life cycle and behaviour of the crocodile. Crocodile Dundee types are always pre-emptive and pro-active. They are pleasant guys to talk to until they spot a badly behaving crocodile whereupon they switch mentally and step in to sort the reptile out.

The Carer The second example of the correct attitude that needs to be displayed by door supervisors is a caring attitude. This is where the door supervisors believe that they are there to care for and protect all the customers, staff and property.

This attitude has to be maintained, even when the customers and staff appear to be going obnoxious or reptile. As soon as you lose sight of the caring factor, you are neck deep in doggy do.

When a young person sets their mind on having a good night out, you are there to protect them and ensure that they do have a good night out. You are there to greet them into your venue and then bid them 'Safe Home' at the end of the night. Between those two events, you are there to protect them, even from their own excesses. Show them, when necessary, the acceptable limits of their behaviour and inform them about the 'House Rules'. Verbally and physically abusing naive young people is not a door supervisor task. Caring for them is.

Psychological research has shown that your attitude will be more consistently reflected in your behaviour if you are incorporating the following three factors.

- You have to be totally involved in learning the social and physical skills of the door supervisor

- The knowledge and information you acquire on the duties of a door supervisor will positively affect your behaviour

- Direct experience acquired in working the door will also positively affect your behaviour

Personality Type

The second psychological factor that affects the behaviour of the door supervisor is their personality type. There are four personality types of interest to the door supervisor and their employers.

Hans Eysenck and the Three Personality Types In 1981, The British psychologist Hans Eysenck described how the normal population fits into three distinct personality types. These are, extroversion-introversion, instability-stability and psychoticism-superego. In reality, most individuals are a mixture of all the personality types, with different personality types being expressed at different times.

The psychotic traits of hostility and insensitivity to others are just as detrimental to keeping the peace as the instability traits. These will cause the door supervisor to overreact in stressful situations. Introverts will also cause havoc in a stressful situation by withdrawing from the scene. So, introversion, instability and psychoticism are unsuitable personality types for any security work.

There is only one type of personality suitable for the job of door supervisor work. The social interactive role of the door supervisor demands the personality of the extrovert. This gregarious person is defined as someone who enjoys meeting and interacting with others. The door supervisor must always be capable of verbally expressing him or herself. On other occasions the door supervisor may need to empathise with others to control the situation. This task appears to be easier for extroverts as opposed to introverts who bottle up their feelings and may allow a situation to deteriorate without speaking out.

The Psychopath The fourth personality type found in the abnormal population has been called the psychopath or sociopath. The psychopath is always concerned with short-term gains. They try to control individuals for their own personal gain and are incapable of empathizing with others.

When a psychopath attempts to control a situation and fails, they become more easily frustrated and therefore inclined to be more physically aggressive, impulsive and reckless. The psychopath is also incapable of considering the consequences of their behaviour or learning from their mistakes. The egocentric orientation of the psychopath's social interaction skills will not allow them to sustain a long-term influence over regular customers.

Individuals with a high score in these four personality types described above; introversion, instability, psychoticism and psychopathy have to be weeded out in the initial stages of training, perhaps with an aptitude tick test. To put an individual without basic security training or the correct psychological profile in charge of the security and well-being of a venue crowd is about as sensible as giving a monkey a loaded gun.

Moral Courage

The third psychological factor that affects the behaviour of the door supervisor is their moral courage. This is the type of courage that allows you to think rationally in tight situations and respond with good as opposed to evil behaviour.

It is not everybody who can handle both physical and verbal abuse without over-reacting. Psychopaths and other individuals may not have the moral fibre to stand up and achieve their objectives in the face of contempt, violence and interference.

The long-term method of developing this rational mind set would be from constant personal experience with all the mistakes up front to slow down the learning process.
The ideal way to test and develop moral courage is to be placed in a training scenario that replicates the real world. That way you will develop an attitude that is reflected in your behaviour because the attitude is based on practical experience and knowledge.

Training Door Supervisors to Deal With Psychological Stress

Real life scenario training is essential for door supervisors who must learn to respond to the psychological factors that could affect their behaviour. This form of training has these three main objectives.
First, the training must be constructed to weed out those individuals who are totally incapable of coping with both verbal and physical abuse.
Second, the training must develop the correct attitude in the individual so that the attitude is reflected in their behaviour.
Third, the training must be progressive in nature so that it builds up the physical and social skills of the door supervisor under instruction. This form of training would also have the effect of inuring the door supervisor to the effects of both verbal and physical abuse.

At present the UK and US national approach to the training of door supervisors has been restricted to knowledge based assessment tests. Sometimes door supervisors are now registered to care for the protection of the customers at their venue, based on their response to a tick test. In the real world the demands will shift from this tick test of knowledge and literacy to the practical skills of verbal and non-verbal interaction as well as physical control. These areas have not been addressed adequately in the training programmes.

The Sources of Violence

Many different factors have been cited for aggression at licensed venues. These factors include; heat, noise, overcrowding, alcohol, anger,

fear, pain, and finally, aggressive cues such as available weapons or improvised weapons.
I have found that these factors are triggers that induce violence. The prime factor for aggression at venues appears to be incompatibility.

- When incompatibility exists between the aspirations, goals and expectancies of customers and door staff there will be trouble

- Incompatibility can also exist between customers from different cultures and social groups

- Incompatibility exists when individual behaviour becomes unacceptable to others

Violent Conflict Between Customers and Door Supervisors

Outlined next are five main causes for violent conflict between customers and door supervisors:

- Violent intent of the customer

- Emotional instability of the door supervisor

- Lack of door supervisor training in social interaction skills

- Alcohol

- Frustration - Aggression Theory

Violent Intent of the Customer

On many occasions a door supervisor will be confronted by a customer, either drunk or sober who is hell bent on starting a fight. This violent customer will blank out all the de-escalation efforts of the door supervisor and continue to go 'reptile'.
The two main types of aggression used by customers on door supervisors are labelled Instrumental and Emotional.
Instrumental aggression is the form of aggression used to eliminate the victim. In this situation an individual confronting you is totally committed to making your face resemble a busted sofa.

As another example, the bar may contain at least ten regulars whom you have 'spoken to' or put down on earlier occasions. They will take the opportunity of a row or fight to sneak in a naughty poke or two on your blind side and then give you a bad beating.

People experiencing extreme anger or fear use emotional aggression. They may be angry because you will not allow them into the venue so they vent their rage on you. On other occasions, the customer may be trying to start a fight with another customer. When the door supervisors step in to de-escalate the situation, the violent customer becomes angrier. Without warning, the door supervisors then become the target.

Fear may induce emotional aggression. For example, while you are escorting a person off the venue, they may attack you because they fear for their safety. Some venues have a bad reputation for escorting customers outside to give them a kicking off camera. If this is what a customer expects, you will have trouble escorting them off the premises.

Again, their legal representatives may cite the 'Twinkie Clause', the 'Abuse Excuse' or the 'Drunk as a Skunk' clause for their deplorable lapse, but the door supervisors can only interpret what they are faced with as violent intent and then protect themselves.

Emotional Instability of the Door Supervisor

The door supervisor needs a high standard in emotional stability. It is their primary role to care for all the individuals at their venue. It is also the duty of the door supervisor to remain impervious to the slings and arrows from toe rags trying to goad them into unprofessional modes of behaviour. Once the door supervisor starts taking insults as a personal slight, they become emotionally involved in the situation and it rapidly escalates into a physical confrontation.

Two examples of emotionally unstable types are the submissive and the angry.

Mister Mumbles the Submissive The submissive behaviour of Mr. Mumbles the door supervisor can be problematic. Because of his inability to articulate his objectives or interact with the customer the problem is going to remain unresolved. He will look down, apologize and back away, leaving the problem for some other team member to sort out. Perhaps Mr. Mumbles will overcompensate for his inarticulate nature with some frustrated aggression by whacking the problem customer.

Mister Angry the Aggressive Just like submissive behaviour, aggressive behaviour must be avoided. For example, your partner Mr Angry will create problems by behaving like the Reptile. Observe him stabbing out his finger to emphasise every word he is screaming at the customer in front of him. He is creating a situation by shouting out orders at the customer and leaving no room for a compromise.

The problem is going to accelerate and Mr. Angry will resolve it with his fists. If you were observing two customers, you would have to throw out Mr. Angry.

Lack of Door Supervisor Training in Social Interaction Skills

The aim of the door supervisor is to keep violent behaviour from occurring at all, not just responding to or controlling it. Learning how to walk, talk, stand and interact with others is a small price to pay for a peaceful night's work.

Learning how to de-escalate violent situations will reduce the chance of those situations escalating at all. It is far better to experience insulting behaviour in the confines of the training environment than in the real world. A hasty response to a 'term of endearment' will cost the door supervisor his job and sometimes his house.

Once the anatomy of bum fights are explained to an individual, (In the next book, The Door Supervisor: The Physical Skills by Ronnie Gamble) they will be much better equipped, both mentally and emotionally, to respond to the fight in a professional manner.

Alcohol

This is a legal drug that attacks and anaesthetizes the fore brain. This part of the brain is responsible for all aspects of learning, judgement, the regulation of behaviour (Scarf 1976 p. 87), speech and memory.

Alcohol will also make individuals hypersensitive to aggressive cues, either real or imagined. Consider this section from a table of statistics issued by The Health Promotion Agency (NI, 2002), where alcohol has been estimated to be a factor in:

- 45% of wounding and assault cases

- 88% of criminal damage arrests

But alcohol may not be the culprit at the core of all violence or dysfunctional behaviour. Many drunken people will lose their power of speech or just fall asleep rather than engage in violent behaviour. The percentages above also show that most of the population do not need the use of alcohol to become involved in violent acts against others.

Frustration - Aggression Theory

Frustration occurs when someone, deliberately or accidentally, stops another individual from achieving an objective. This frustration, in turn, will lead to aggression. For example, you may deny someone access to your venue. The individual feels that they are close to achieving their goal and they become frustrated. An argument follows because they have been denied access and the door supervisor then becomes the focus of their rage.

Chapter 4

Basic Duties

Door supervisors are primarily tasked with maintaining security and safety at the venue. This includes the property, the staff and all the customers at the venue.

The basic duties of the door supervisor include:

- Dealing with problems created through the consumption of alcohol

- Meeting, greeting, interacting with and bidding farewell to all customers

- Helping all customers with any queries they may have

- Dealing with the problems of age, searching customers and denying entry

- Reacting positively in emergency situations that may endanger customers, staff or property

To carry out these basic duties in a professional and non-discriminatory manner, door supervisors should be trained in the following basic skills. These skills will be covered in more detail throughout this work:

- Drug Awareness

- Effects of Alcohol Consumption

- Assessing Customer Profiles

- Disability Awareness, Etiquette and Courtesy

- Dress and Package Search Procedures

- Risk Assessment
- Conflict Resolution and De-escalation Skills
- Control and Restraint
- Dealing with Drunken Customers
- Basic Radio Procedure
- Team Work

Preparation

Good preparation before your duty starts will help you to function properly throughout your time on duty. Remember that your primary duty is to take care of, help and ensure the safety of the customers and staff. This mind set will keep you in the correct mood to carry out your duty.

Also consider the view that the last, and never to be forgotten, option to exercise is hitting out. This will help you to cope much better with the day-to-day running of the door and the floor. Instead of having a paranoid outlook to the job, you will develop a more friendly and approachable disposition.

Other than the radio, pen, spare pen and notebook, and your personal set of house keys to let yourself in at 2am, consider the following points in your preparation.

Food

The condemned man or woman must eat a hearty meal to sustain them on their long night vigil. If you are too anxious to eat then you are too anxious to do the job.

Identification

Always carry details of your local G.P./M.D., Legal Aid, Blood Group, your address and contact numbers of your relatives.

Clothing

Wear clean underwear and clothing. You may have to go to hospital or a police cell later that evening for an indeterminate period. Clean clothing will protect you if clothing enters a fresh flesh wound. If the weather is cold, consider wearing black pyjama bottoms below your trousers. If you want to keep your reactions sharp and your body comfortable, then always dress to cope with the weather. Wear steel toe-capped shoes for your own protection. They must also have good insulation to keep out the cold, as well as a non-slip sole that grips well on vomit, glass, shite, blood and spilled beer.

First Aid

Carry a small flat tin box or pouch containing some first aid plasters, a pair of surgical gloves for incidents involving blood and vomit, resuscitation face shield, alcohol wipes and plasters. Nitrile gloves (usually the blue ones) tend to be a bit harder wearing and less prone to splitting when putting them on in a hurry (Mulholland, Graham. 2009). Have a pair of pre-threaded needles of black and white thread.

Quick Repair Kit

Carry spare clothing for the job and have it close by. After a minor fracas you will look ridiculous standing on the door without your jacket sleeves. It is best that the needles are pre-threaded because after an emotionally disturbing incident you will have the shakes and limited coordination. Last, but essential, carry a personal supply of headache tablets.

Extra Fuel and Comfort Eating

One pocket carries a small supply of chocolate and shortbread biscuits. After an early evening meal this supply boosts your blood sugar levels and heats up your body. Carrying these aids will ensure that you have no reason to wander off looking for snacks.
OK... so there is another reason for carrying some form of food, it is this. Throughout the night you will have to address many different and stressful situations. The side effect will be a dry mouth. Carrying a quick bite of confectionery will help to get the saliva running again and thus accelerate your calming down process.

Avoid the use of chewing gum. Always remember that the body language of the untrained always mirrors their inner feelings. Stress will make you chew gum like a maniac. This is very comical looking to those in the know.

Creating Positive Impressions

When customers enter or leave a venue, their first and last contact is with the door supervisor. The reputation, conviviality and feel good factors the customers take away from a venue are largely determined through their interactions with the door supervisor.
Always create a good impression by maintaining high standards in your dress, appearance, language and conduct during all phases of your duties. Pay attention to the following basic requirements and this will help to reduce your workload throughout the night and also the workload of your head supervisor.

Looking Good List

- Hair combed
- Clean/pressed shirt/suit
- No foul or lewd language
- Steel toe-capped shoes polished
- No rings, brass or medallions, (man)
- Keep smiling at the appropriate times
- Keep your head up and look at all the customers
- Greet all the customers, not just those you fancy
- Physically cover the door to keep out the rubbish
- Open the door for all the customers you are allowing into the venue

House Rules

The House Rules will include codes of dress. For example base ball caps and hooded jackets may be banned because they offer a degree of anonymity to the wearer who may go on to start trouble and remain unidentified. Without the baseball cap or hooded jacket, the security cameras can pick out the troublemakers in action. This way, the legal process can go on. Other items on the hit list must include anything that would cause offence to other customers. This includes sports tops, political emblems and street gang colours.

The Customer

The reputation of any venue is dependent on more than its décor, layout, size and behaviour of the bar staff and supervisors. The reputation of the venue will also be determined by the behaviour of the customers. When a person enters a venue to drink alcohol, they are also bringing their mood, their environment, their prejudices, their habits and their upbringing with them. All these factors can be disguised by their dress and response to your initial greeting at the door. In this section I will discuss assessing customers, deciding who is denied access and how to refuse admission to a customer.

Assessing Customers

It is the duty of the door staff to ensure that anyone entering their venue is filtered from the criteria set out in the next section.
Years spent developing the good reputation of any venue can be undermined by one bad incident that traumatises customers. By denying access to known disreputable characters you will help to maintain all the 'feel good' factors of your venue.
There will always be occasions when you assess someone, consider them to be OK and allow them on the premises. Then you find them taking a leading part in an ugly incident later on.
Always hold a post mortem on anything that goes wrong. You are not looking for someone to blame; you are looking to see how the person became involved in the incident and if there was any mistake in your assessment of the customer on their initial approach. That is how you will build up your experience in social interaction and customer assessment.

Denying Access

You will be responsible for denying access to individuals or groups who:

- Refuse to be searched

- Are known drug dealers

- Refuse to pay the entrance fee

- Are under the legal age for drinking

- May be drunk or under the influence of drugs

- Do not conform to the dress code of your venue

- Are male or female prostitutes, plying their trade

- Are unable to produce a valid proof of age document

- May cause the venue to exceed the legal crowd capacity

- Clearly have an attitude problem that may distress other customers

- Have a reputation for disruptive behaviour, criminal behaviour or have been already barred

The Refusal

When you refuse entry to an individual or group, this action may lead to a problem. This is particularly true if you do not give a clear explanation for your actions. You must use social interaction skills that defuse the situation. Remain calm, keep your hands open and above waist level and explain clearly your reasons for refusing entry. The refusal is based on the unprejudiced application of the House Rules and not your personal interpretation of them. As a last resort, close the door but when you refuse entry to an unwanted customer, try this first:

- Remaining polite and calm

- Explaining the House Rules

- Calling the Head Supervisor or Duty Bar Manager, if necessary, to support your stance

- Calling for back up, if necessary. Do this by pressing the send button and transmitting part of the conversation, using code words e.g., 'This bar'. This alerts the back up but not the person you are refusing access, who may hit and run before the back up arrives

The Door Supervisor's Tasks

Your Safety and Security tasks are always carried out in three phases, Pre-Event, Event and Post-Event. Some of the tasks mentioned for each stage are not specific to that one stage alone. Several of the items mentioned in these lists will be expanded on later. There will be occasions when you will be tasked to operate inside the venue as a floor supervisor. These tasks have also been included here.

Pre-Event Safety and Security

- Check in ten minutes before your job starts

- Sign the Incident Book and check to see who is barred from entering your location

- Sign out radios, learn the call signs and carry out radio checks

- Check all the rooms for vandalism, rubbish, floor debris, lost property, suspicious packages or any slip and trip hazards

- Check all the seating for damage and fresh chewing gum, anything that can turn an old suit into an Armani when it comes to compensation

- Check that all fire exits; the routes to them and the area outside your venue is free from obstructions

- Check that the emergency opening bars on the emergency exit doors are operating and are not locked or chained

- Check that all fire extinguishers are in position, visible and the seals are not broken

- Review the house rules on admissions and search procedures

- Ask the bar manager if the security cameras are on and recording

- Ask the bar manager what the legal maximum crowd capacity of the venue is

- Check that the Sin Bin/Honesty Box for banned articles is in position. This must be accompanied with bags and labels for banned items you have found during a search

- Know if/where there is a sharps disposal bin

- Learn where all the out of bounds areas are for you and the customers

- Any problems? Report them in the incident book and inform your head supervisor

- Familiarise yourself with all the information customers expect you to give them

Event Safety and Security

- Stay at your post unless moved by the Head Supervisor

- Monitor queues to ensure good order. Do not allow queue jumpers to gain access to the event. The animosity they created outside can spill over inside the event

- Speak to people in the queue. Offer advice and let them know what is happening. This is the stage to establish a good rapport with the customers and identify the 'tossers'

- Be familiar with the age limits on drinking and legal ID systems

- Search all backpacks, large bags and handbags if necessary. It all depends on the terrorist threat level

- Ask all pack carrying customers to store their packs below their seats so that they do not become a trip hazard

- Be familiar with the House Rules and enforce them intelligently without causing embarrassment to the customers

- Always be able to account for the numbers present at your venue. Too many customers will lead to over-crowding and slow service at the counters. This situation can lead to frustration and aggressive responses to minor incidents. It is also a health and safety hazard if there are too many customers for the staff to cope with if an emergency occurs

- When customers are leaving the venue, ensure that they are not taking any souvenirs. This includes fire extinguishers, glasses, ashtrays and bottles or any other item that can be used as a weapon. You may be held liable for any injuries sustained by a customer who injures themselves or others with an item you obviously allowed them to remove from the venue

- Ensure that all pack carriers leave your venue with their packs. By engaging them in conversation on their entry and also searching them, you are more likely to remember them as they leave

- Watch out for customers who may not be drunk, but under the influence of rape drugs. Always stop and question the person who may be innocently escorting or perhaps abducting them off your venue. Ask the escorts for their ID, you may be saving a life

Ticket Only Venues

Ticket only venues have their own unique set of problems. Most of these problems can be avoided by following a few simple rules. Ignore these rules at your peril.

- Check every ticket for the date and entrance number

- Never ask the customer, 'Is this ticket for...?' Always check the ticket. The customer may be at the wrong entrance or may be trying to bluff you

- Never leave the door to sort out a query; this creates a bigger problem

- Stay tight to the door so that no one enters the venue without your permission

- Refer all problems to the Head Supervisor

- Accept no excuse from individuals with either the incorrect or no ticket at all

Post Event Safety and Security

- Sign in the radios, and report any breakages or problems

- Check all seating and rest rooms for rubbish, floor debris, lost property and suspicious packages

- Check all seating for fresh chewing gum. It's amazing how expensive it is to clean up an old suit

- Check that there are no smouldering cigarettes lying about

- Check that all fire exits, the routes to them and the area outside your venue is free from obstruction

- Check that all fire extinguishers are in position and the seals are not broken

- Carry out a systematic building check, including the toilets and other small rooms leading off the venue area to confirm that the building is clear of all customers

- Any incidents? Report them in the incident book and inform your head supervisor. (More details later)

- Any contraband in the Sin Bin/Honesty Box? If so, inform the local police that the bin is full and they will come and empty it

The Floor Supervisor's Tasks

Floor Duties

Variety is the spice of life. After a stint on the door it is a relief to be switched to floor duties. Always try to stay one jump ahead of the bar manager and your Head Supervisor. The best indicator that you may be 'switched off' or inexperienced is when the bar manager comes up to you and passes barbed comments, such as:

- 'They are smoking in the back hall'

- 'Wake that guy up'

- 'The main walk way at the top of the stairs is blocked with people'

- 'How did they get in?'

A good head supervisor or bar manager with access to a bank of security cameras may be keeping a tight eye on all activities at your venue. If you think you can switch off and bluff it for a while, a good head supervisor or bar manager will soon spot your omissions and shake you down.

Your floor duties will include responsibility for the security and safety of the:

- Bar Staff

- Floor Staff

- Customers

- Building

Bar Staff Security and Safety Continually ask the bar staff and waiters if everything is OK. That way you will get to sort out any events long before the bar manager is informed. That approach also gives you the opportunity to go in and sort out an event before it deteriorates. The bar staff will be subject to verbal and physical abuse as the night goes on. By asking about their safety, you are offering them mutual support.

When the bar staff are not under pressure from a packed house, they have more time to spot those customers over the limit. If they refuse to serve this type of customer they may need your support. This is because such an event is fraught with danger for them, as the drunken customer can turn belligerent. You must always keep the bar staff under observation to protect them.

The waiter service needs a clear pathway around the venue. Make sure their main routes are not jammed with groups congregating in inappropriate areas. This includes areas near or on the stairs and at the bar staff (Service) counter.

Floor Staff Security and Safety   Always position yourself so that you are within visual contact of other floor staff. This action provides mutual support. You may notice an event about to take place in their blind spot. Serious incidents are usually infrequent. When something goes down, you can leave your spot and back up other staff. The stronger you are numerically at the incident, the less likely it will be to escalate.

If you spot a fight starting, always inform your team by radio and give them the exact location of the fight area. Always wait for those who are available to respond before moving in. Never go into a fight alone.

Customer Security and Safety   Sometimes bar staff will be poorly trained and will continue to serve customers who are clearly over the limit. When you first come on duty you have to check all the customers for this state and inform the bar staff to stop serving before you eject the drunken customer.

If a customer becomes drunk, they may want to sleep. Do not allow this to happen, they are apt to fall over or even be robbed. After two warnings, escort them off the premises. In some countries, drunken individuals are not allowed to remain in bars. Always appeal to the friends of the drunken person before removing them.

You have a duty of care to all the customers at your venue. What will you do with an individual who is falling over drunk? The taxi service will not transport drunken passengers, as they are apt to 'throw up' over the interior. They will damage the reputation of that venue if you leave them lying around the front entrance. Do you take some mother's son to the nearest alley where they can be arrested, robbed, murdered, raped, mugged or asphyxiated on their vomit?

If you allow a customer to drink too much before asking them to leave, there is the additional threat to the venues drinking licence at the next review. It is this, the drunken customer may become a victim to a falling injury and this event will be logged by the local police and presented at the next licence review board.

Keep talking to the customers and assess their needs. By using a friendly approach you will help to explode the old myths about door and floor staff.

Once customers become aware that you are there for their security and safety they will open up and inform you about anything that is amiss. For example, they may inform you about arguments in the toilet area that could develop into something more serious.

Always keep your area clear of broken furniture, broken glasses and unused cutlery. These items may act as cues for aggressive behaviour. Berkowitz (1968) noted weapons may stimulate acts of violence.

> 'Guns not only permit violence, they can stimulate it as well. The finger pulls the trigger, but the trigger may also be pulling the finger' (p. 22).

When a spillage occurs, you must stand in the immediate area to deny access to customers. Always call the bar staff to clean up the spillage. At this stage you must remain in close to the bar staff so that they can clean up without customers walking through the hazard.

Be vigilant for anything that may cause annoyance or distress for the customers. For example, over-boisterous behaviour or foul language from other groups will upset the ambience of the venue.

Be vigilant for suspicious or furtive behaviour. This includes drug dealing activities, terrorists planting devices or the spiking of drinks with rape drugs.

On some occasions, children may be allowed into the dining area of your venue. This will present another unique set of problems. It is likely that they will become restless and start to roam about. You have to be patient and never allow the children to become a danger to themselves or others. Also become familiar with the predatory behaviour patterns of the paedophile.

In an emergency, children, people with special needs and others with impairments will have to be given special consideration. Always know where these individuals are located. Become familiar with your venue rules for actions in any emergency.

Building Security and Safety Be on the lookout for suspicious packages. When a customer leaves a spot in your area, have they left anything behind? This analysis of and reaction to everyday occurrences must become second nature to you. Perhaps they innocently left their package behind.

During your duty, all damaged or insecure furniture and glass must be removed for the comfort and safety of the customers.

Always intervene when someone interferes with fire doors or fire fighting equipment.

Do not allow bar staff to clutter up fire exits or fire fighting equipment with empty kegs and other bar wastage. These routes will be needed for emergency evacuations and ejections of unruly customers. If security doors and fire doors are supposed to be closed, ensure this is happening.

Check that all fire exits; the routes to them and the areas outside the fire exits are free from obstructions.

Spot the Fire Appliance in the Emergency Exit?

Physical Positioning and Manipulation

You must control the movement of customers entering your venue. This is done through a combination of correct physical positioning, appropriate questioning and finally, vigilant observation.

The exact spot you place yourself in for each task is critically important. Correct physical positioning is the final arbitrator between total control and total chaos. The correct position always depends on the type of venue and the structural design.

The following pointers will help to explain these factors and may eliminate the distress of learning through error.

On the Door

At the start of the night, you have to be close to the door to control the customers entering the venue. It is important to remember always that if you are physically covering the door, there will be no opportunity for the gatecrasher to get into the premises without physically assaulting you.

If you accidentally allow any form of rubbish into the premises, you will have to chase after them and then go physical to get their attention. It will prove less embarrassing to stop this from happening through good cover on the door.

Early   Late

At the end of the evening, you must position yourself towards the outer door. This allows you to stop customers leaving the venue with glasses, bottles, fire extinguishers or any other item that must remain on the premises. This procedure will stop you from having to chase after customers and going hands on to halt them. This is a situation fraught with problems.

Manoeuvring

Being restricted to covering the door reduces all your options for coping with a troublesome customer.
Customers may try to line you up and strike you. I call it dirty dancing. The indicators are short rapid breaths, dancing about, freezing their breathing and a glazed eye expression.
Without leaving the door you can screw up their plans by adjusting your stance and maintaining eye contact. The phrase, 'Don't even think about it' is the final nail in their coffin.

Outside Events

At some events, fixed fencing as well as stewards may separate rival groups. It is important that you place yourself at least arms length away from the fencing. This denies anybody on the other side of the fence the opportunity to grab and pull you into the fencing.

The Fence

At some pop concerts, the fencing is more mobile and flexible. It is primarily used to channel the customers as opposed to containing them. You must position yourself further away from this form of fencing. This is because any social cretin who decides to shoulder charge the fencing will crash it into you.

Basic Radio Procedure

When all radio users are using the same basic set of procedures, the communications system will sound much more professional. On too many occasions, the radio procedures used by individuals reflect the bad habits used by actors on TV cop shows.
When you are issued with a radio there are five sets of facts that you must know. This knowledge will help to make you a more competent radio user and most important of all, the system will also be more user friendly.

The Channel

The radio must be set to the correct channel. All radio operators carrying out the same job must ensure they are on the same channel.

The Volume

It must be set correctly so that you can hear all messages above the background noise.

The Call Signs

All operators must know the call signs being used that day. You must be able to identify the radio user by their call sign.

The Protocol

Press the send button- Pause for half of a second - Speak - Keep the message short. Listen in always, someone may be trying to contact you.

Table 4: The Message Procedure

Procedure	What you are doing	What you say
Radio Check	Call sign Alpha is calling Bravo.	Hello Bravo this is Alpha, Radio Check, Over.
	Bravo acknowledges the check	Bravo, OK, Over.
	Alpha acknowledges the check.	Alpha, OK, Out.
Sending a Message	Call sign Alpha calls up Bravo.	Hello Bravo this is Alpha, Over.
	Bravo acknowledges the call.	Bravo, Send, Over.
	Alpha sends the message.	Alpha, (Send the full message) Over.
	Bravo acknowledges the message.	Bravo, Roger, Over.
	Alpha ends the message.	Alpha, Out.

Disability Awareness

Introduction

As a professional door supervisor it is important that you learn how to interact positively with all the customers at your venue so that they have a positive attitude towards that venue.

You must learn how to behave in a non-discriminatory manner with the customers. Interact with everyone with some degree of empathy for their religion, politics, gender orientation, sex, sexual preferences, race, age and finally, their physical and mental abilities.

Inappropriate comments or behaviour can lead to misunderstandings that may ruin the reputation of your venue. For example, there have been instances of people being ejected for drunkenness simply because:

- They were partially sighted and had lost their cane

- A person with slurred speech and a mobility problem due to a stroke

- A diabetic with an insulin problem was falling asleep

In this section, I will introduce the basic information you will need in order to interact and behave properly with individuals who have a disability.

People with disabilities are not one stereotypical group that can be addressed in a standardised manner. Again, they are similar to all other customers, with their own particular needs. You have to learn how to interact with all customers and their form of disability so that you do not;

- Behave inappropriately or discriminate

- Simply freeze because of your ignorance about a particular disability

- Ignore the individual

Definition

A customer with a disability or impairment is, in the first instance, a person. Do not talk about "the handicapped" or "the deaf " but do learn to talk about "the wheelchair user" or "the person who is slightly deaf" or "the hearing impaired". Make a point of always prefixing your description of a person with a disability with the phrase "A person with a (Specify the condition) impairment".

A disability may be a result of an accident, genetics, disease or a stroke and this can affect individuals either mentally or physically. For example, someone suffering from the after effects of a stroke may have difficulties in speaking, understanding, reading or writing, handling money or telling the time.

Approximately 20% of any Western Hemisphere population have an impairment that stops them functioning to the same extent as the remaining 80%. This inability to take a fully functional role in their community or society is, in part, due to the restrictions and handicaps placed by society itself. This includes:

- Poor disability awareness training for the general population who remain prejudiced and ignorant with stereotypical views on impairments

- Failure to use common sense while interacting with individuals who have any form of impairment. For example, refusing to allow guide dogs into some venues

- No staff training on the subject of dealing with customers who have disabilities which leads to misunderstandings and embarrassment

- Lack of training facilities or trainers in the workplace to cater for individuals with disabilities

- Inadequate facilities at venues for wheelchair users, i.e. no user friendly toilets, difficult access to the front of the stage, no emergency escape procedures, narrow doorways, steps rather than ramps, emergency exits clogged with rubbish and on and on and on

Some Examples of Poor Disability Awareness

   Get up and Walk   Take a Chance   Struggle Alone

   Blocked Exits   Ambiguous Signs

Forms of Disability

People with disabilities have varying degrees and forms of disability. In some cases, an individual may have several disabilities, these disabilities include:

- Physical or mobility impairments

- Physical disfigurements

- Total blindness or vision impairments

- Profound deafness or hearing impairments

- Speech or language impairment

- Cognitive, developmental or learning disabilities and learning difficulties

Disability Etiquette

People with disabilities have as much right as anyone else to attend any social function. But all too often many people are unable to exercise this right because the venue is not structured or staffed to cater with some forms of disability.

If you have a situation where you are unsure of what to do, consult either the head supervisor or duty bar manager, if you have the time, that is. Always remember you are dealing with a person who has feelings and personal needs, if you are really unsure, ask them directly for advice.

Customers who look and behave differently from the norm can find the experience of facing the general public a traumatic experience. Some of the population will have either physical disfigurements or cognitive impairments. They may have been born with their condition or it may result from a serious illness, an operation or an accident.

You must have the skill to see beyond the surface to see the real person and understand their wants, needs, fears and real personality.

This section is a common sense short-list for dealing with all customers at your venue, not just those with physical or cognitive impairments.

Dealing With all Customers

1. Interact with everyone visiting your venue and help to make their stay enjoyable

2. Identify yourself to the person you are addressing as early as possible

3. Listen to what the person is saying and respond positively

4. Look for cues that identify any particular impairment. This will include wheelchairs, white canes, lapel badges or guide dogs

5. Always address directly the person you have to communicate with, not their friends or care giver

6. Never ignore someone, simply because of his or her impairment or appearance

7. Do not patronise, stare, talk loudly, lose your patience or turn into a comedian. Always act normally. Do not act overtly friendly, paternalistic or condescending with individuals who have any form of impairment

8. Do ask the customers what they prefer, need or want if necessary. You may be doing it all wrong

9. Allow extra time for the person to respond to your questions or greetings

10. Do not make the customer feel uncomfortable. Always act naturally

11. The individual's physical appearance always disguises their true personality

12. Get down to eye level whenever possible and use your normal body language and verbal language

13. Never risk or compromise your personal security or moral standards by becoming isolated with children or a person with impairments. Always remain in the public view

14. Offer a chair if the customer is expected to wait about your area. This also applies to the elderly and the pregnant

Dealing with Customers who have Specific Impairments

Always remember that this is only a short introduction to disability awareness. For example, visual impairment can be further sub-categorised to include total blindness, visual impairment and visual processing impairment and other conditions. This sub-categorisation can be applied to all branches of disability and a description of the full coping procedures would require further volumes.

Wheelchair Users

- Do not lean or stand on the wheelchair or walking frame Always respect the personal space and property of others

- Some wheelchairs are motor assisted. Do not assume the customer has to be pushed

- Always ask the customer if they want you to push their wheelchair

- Make sure there is a clear path of travel

- When addressing a wheelchair pusher to go to a specific place, do not say, "Please take your wheelchair to." They are not taking an object (their wheelchair) to a specific door, they are most likely taking the person they love/their friend (in a wheelchair) to a specific place

Cognitive Impairment

- If the person has a cognitive impairment and are lost, afraid, distressed or disorientated, check their clothing for name and address tags

The Visually Impaired

- If it is necessary for you to escort a blind customer, allow that person to hold your arm, or place your upper arm close to theirs so that they can follow your lead

- Give the customer verbal information about the environment you are moving through and always let them know when you leave their company

The Hearing Impaired

- If the customer is deaf, always position yourself so that your face is well lit for the customer

- Always look directly at the customer and speak clearly without shouting

- Keep your hands away from your mouth and this will allow the person to lip read

- If a person addressing you has a speech impediment and you do not understand what they are saying, ask them to repeat themselves

Chapter 5

Searching

As a searcher you are vulnerable to attack. This is because you are focused on the individual you are searching. Always have someone covering your back. This reduces the risk of someone attacking you or trying to pass without submitting to a search. There should also be a three-bin system in operation at any venue, the Honesty Box/Sin Bin, The Sharps Bin and The Glass Bin.

The Bin System

The Honesty Box/Sin Bin

A well-placed Honesty Box/Sin Bin acts as a deterrent. It is either used or the individual refuses to use it and leaves the venue. The Honesty Bin/Sin Bin should be locked and the key retained by the local police.
The Honesty Box/Sin Bin is a dumping box for illegal or dangerous items. That includes any form of weapon or anything that would endanger the safety of other customers or illegal drugs. Some customers may be unaware of the threat posed by certain items and will have to be made aware of the danger. Any item that goes in will not be returned and that has to be made clear to the customer you are addressing.

The Sharp's Bin

There should be a Sharp's bin available for the disposal of syringe needles.

The Glass Bin

If a glass collector is not present, fill the rubbish bin. A separate bin should be used for glass containers, food, drink and alcohol. That includes any items the customer tries to bring in or take out from your venue. Licensed premises are permitted to sell drink for consumption on the premises. A customer must not be allowed to take their drink off the premises.

After relieving the customer of the bottle or glass, you have to secure that item. It is simple negligence to pile the floor or stairwell with discarded glasses and bottles. This reduces the chance of the item from being used as a weapon and also prevents other customers falling on the discarded bottles and glasses and injuring themselves.

Dress Search Procedure

To emphasise the limitations of door supervisor search procedures that procedure is classed as Dress Search and not Body Search. Searches are carried out as part of your responsibilities for the safety of the staff, the customers and the building.

All customers using your venue must be made aware of your powers of search and powers of seizure under your local government's current and active legislation. This should be clearly displayed at all entrances to your venue.

Most individuals have a positive attitude towards searches. They feel that the more people that are searched, the safer the venue will be. Random searches carried out at the door will act as a deterrent to someone approaching the venue with illicit materials in their possession.

Searches are also an effective way of managing a crowd by slowing them down as they rush the building.

Should a person refuse to give permission for you to search them, deny them access to the venue.

If you attempt to search a person without first gaining their permission, you are apt to be prosecuted for assault. The current threat and what you are looking for will determine your search method.

The aim of all searching is to ensure that no weapons, drugs or other items are carried into the venue that would:

- Spoil the event for other customers

- Create a hazard for other customers

- Create circumstances where the management would be liable to prosecution

- Injure or harm you

An offensive weapon is defined as:

- An item manufactured to cause injury. E.g. baton, knife, knuckleduster, rice flails, gun, etc.

- An item adapted to cause injury. E.g. Baseball caps with razor blades in the peak

- An item that can cause injury. E.G. bar stools, bottles, jugs, etc.

Before you start a search task you must also determine your legal limitations on dress searching. These limitations will include age limits, areas of the body that may be out of bounds and the sex of the subjects. Because searching slows down the movement into the venue it can lead to expressions of frustration and aggression.
There are three types of search, The Visual, The Verbal and The Physical.

The Visual Search

- Long before the subject reaches you, it is important that you check them out visually first. What they are wearing may hide the objects you are after. Are they nervous, sweating or white faced? Perhaps they have been coerced to carry something against their will

- Are they part of a group? Perhaps they are deliberately out to distract you so that the other carriers can slip by

- Is there anything in their gait, stance or posture that is out of the norm?

- The individuals may be carrying banned items openly, unaware that these items are banned

The Verbal Search

- You are still searching the subjects without touching them as yet. By asking questions you may be able to determine their emotional state

- Inform them that you would like them to submit to a search. Refusal at this stage means they will be denied access to the venue. At ticketed events their ticket can be presented at the box office for a refund

- Ask them if they are carrying anything under duress

- Ask them if the have any banned items they would like to dump in the Honesty Box/Sin Bin

The Physical Search

- The more detailed the search, the more embarrassing and intrusive the operation is. The act of searching an individual, even a quick frisk, can be viewed as an infringement of that person's privacy. Be constantly aware of this point and conduct the search with some empathy for the customer

- Searches are conducted without the searcher putting their hands into the subjects' pockets, clothing or containers. This procedure protects you from contact with infected needles. It will also protect you from accusations of theft or the planting of illegal items

The Full Search Sequence

1. When you go hands on in the search, you must be systematic. Do not pat the body. The most sensitive part of the hand is the fingertips. Use them to slide over the body, squeezing and pressing on anything out of place.

2. Always start at the top front and work your way down. Then ask the subject to turn around and repeat the procedure. Remove any headwear and inspect it. Check below the collars of shirts and coats. Check ears, belt lines and the small of the back along the spine.

3. Use metal detectors if these items are available. Practise on one another to develop your skills first.

4. Ask the subject to open their coats, bags, holdalls, parcels etc.

5. If your suspicions are aroused, ask the subject to turn out their pockets so you can search any items produced.

6. If you are suspicious, ask the subject to take closed items out of their containers and open them up.

Actions on a Find

- When you find drugs, they may turn out to be legitimate prescription drugs. You must inform the head supervisor immediately and they will be the final arbitrator on the matter. Some individuals may have a prescribed drug. Unless you are drug awareness trained or have a resident medic competent enough to confirm this, do not confiscate the item

- If any prescribed drug has a label attached, check that the name and address matches the identity of the person you searched. If the details do not correspond then your head supervisor will require further investigative action

- If you suspect that someone is selling drugs within the venue, you must inform the head supervisor immediately or have a member of the venue management present. The rules for dealing with suspect drug dealers vary from country to country. Ask them to come to the main door and submit to a search. Once there, you can either search them with their permission, eject them or arrest them and call the police. If you search them, do it in a side room and in front of the security camera.

- Keep a written record in the occurrence book of each item seized

Evidence Handling and Continuity of Possession

If evidence is to have any validity there must be a proper record of its movement from the scene of the alleged crime to the court of law. The searcher who finds an illicit item must bag and tag the item. The purpose of the tag is to record the times, the journey and all the individuals who have to handle the item before it reaches its final destination.

The fewer people that are involved in this procedure the better. If the evidence handling and continuity of possession is not kept accurate, then the evidence is flawed. The information in the occurrence book concerning a find must include:

- At what time it was seized.

- At what location the item was seized.

- Who was searched? (Name and address/physical description)

- Who carried out the search? (Registration number)

- Who witnessed the search? (The cover man, including their Registration number)

- What the item was

- Why it was seized

- How the item was handled. (Each recipient must complete the item's evidence handling tag with their name, time and date until its final disposal)

Large Venue Search Procedure

In the interest of health and safety there must be two stages to the search procedure. First, the customers must be made aware of items that are not permitted into crowded areas. Second, the customers have to be channelled into a search area where it can be confirmed that they are not attempting to carry in any banned items. Remember, body searches are not permitted; it is only a dress search. Do not put your hands inside the persons clothing or property when you are searching. The banned items will include:

- Any form of weapon

- Any item that can be used as a weapon

- Umbrellas, (eye damage)

- Glass tumblers and bottles, (used as missiles, slip and trip hazard, risk of breaking)

- Plastic bottles with the screw caps still on (remove the screw cap and that will deter, but not stop people from filling the bottle with urine for throwing)

- Cans of any description (used as missiles, slip or trip hazards)

At the first barrier these items should be discarded into a waste bin. When someone arrives at the first barrier, there must be a drinking facility and plastic cups for carrying the drinks into the venue.

At the second stage of the search procedure, males must search only males and females must only search females. Some customers will be very eager to enter the venue and will not mind who searches them. This is a state of mind that will leave them open to sexual assault by an unscrupulous searcher, so the rules must be enforced.

Chapter 6

Drug Awareness

The term 'Club Drugs' refers to illegal substances used by the customers in order to achieve an altered state of consciousness. The mental state achieved can turn out to be unpleasant and the door supervisors may have to deal with the problem. These illegal substances are usually manufactured in conditions of limited hygiene. They may also contain bulking agents unfit for human consumption as well as an indeterminate mix of lethal chemicals. These 'Club Drugs' include Cannabis, MDMA (Ecstasy), Uppers, LSD, Heroin derivatives, Crack, etc.

It is a criminal offence for people to allow their venue to be used for the smoking of cannabis, illegal drugs and the illegal supply of drugs. This includes the occupier of a house or any person responsible for the security or management of a motel, hostel, bar, youth club or nightclub. As a door supervisor you are responsible for taking proactive measures that prevent the sale or use of illegal drugs at your venue.

The Dangers

With the exception of cannabis, 'Club Drugs' are usually colourless, odourless and have no discernable taste. Other than long term mental and physical damage there are some immediate dangers associated with these illegal drugs. Some of the ill effects that occur include seizure, high blood pressure, kidney failure, loss of consciousness, respiratory arrest, convulsions, high body temperature, shaking, confusion, coma, disinhibition, vomiting and sedation. For example, ecstasy will cause the body to overheat. When this happens and there is no access to water, the body will be under-hydrated. In this state the individual is more prone to blood clots and embolisms, which lead to death.

When the person has access to water, there is a danger from drinking too much and over-hydrating the body. This will lead to a swelling of the brain and death. As another example, the use of LSD will lead to serious mental disorders. These include paranoia, sensory distortion, hallucinations and aggressive behaviour.

If there is a bad batch of club drug in circulation expect a major medical problem from affected young people. Do not confuse their condition with excessive alcohol abuse. Do expect overdosing to take place in many cases because home made club drugs have no standard dosage. When a club drug is taken along with an alcoholic drink, the effects are intensified and the mix becomes more lethal.

The Dealers

There are many methods of drug dealing at licensed premises.

1. The independent drug dealer operating on their own

2. Pairs of independent dealers at one venue. One holds the drugs and the other holds the cash

3. Criminal gangs take over the door security and sell drugs

4. Criminal gangs intimidate the door staff to sell drugs

5. Criminal gangs bribe the door staff to sell drugs

6. Criminal gangs bribe the door staff to allow dealers to operate at their venue

7. Criminal gangs intimidate door staff to allow drug dealers to operate at their venue

8. Door staff are paid to hold the drug supply for the dealers operating at their venue

The Cues For Drug Dealing

When you have a resident drug dealer at your venue, their activity will intensify during the festive season, during holidays or when there is an event external to your location. Watch out for any of the following behaviour patterns:

- The dealer may be conducting their business by mobile phone. Expect a constant flow of visitors who do not stay for a drink but walk out of your view

- Watch out for frequent trips to the toilet, beer garden, and car park, off camera, away from your vantage point or other quiet areas where the deal can go down or the drug can be ingested

- The dealer may be 'on edge'. Watch for furtive behaviour patterns that will betray their illegal activity and their fear of being caught

- The dealer may constantly go off the premises to supply an individual from an external cache

- The dealing will intensify about two hours before the external venue kicks off. Under these circumstances you will have groups of young people taking drugs and drinking at your venue in preparation of reaching a 'high' prior to the event

The Tools

Cannabis users will usually have a tobacco tin filled with papers, loose tobacco and a finger sized brown lump of cannabis. Ecstasy tablets are usually individually wrapped in silver foil or small wraps of paper. Heroin derivatives involve the use of small tobacco pipes, burnt silver foil, tightly rolled bank notes and syringes. Never touch syringes, you must learn from your senior supervisor or a qualified medic on how to dispose of these items.

The Physical Cues

To determine if an individual has ingested drugs, you would expect to find some of the following symptoms and indicators:

- Dilated pupils. This is where the iris has expanded from a small black dot in the centre of the eye to a much larger black orb. Some locations have received bad reports because the door staff will spend too long staring the customers in the eye and unnerving them. If the door staff do have a sight impairment, make them wear glasses for this task

- Excessive thirst or excessive hunger. Cannabis will make you hungry and ecstasy will make you thirsty

- Hyperactive or dopey

- White powder (Cocaine) on the nose from sniffing lines of the powder. Cocaine is also smoked or injected

- Cannabis leaves a sweet and musty smell

- Frequent trips to the toilet. This condition is not to be confused by normal alcohol consumption. The more alcohol a person drinks, the more frequently they will visit the toilet. This is nothing to do with the amount of liquid in the bladder. It has more to do with the alcohol affecting the bladders ability to retain urine

- Over friendly or talkative

- Use of lollipops or baby pacifiers to disguise the involuntary teeth grinding caused by MDMA

- Dancers may carry and use brightly coloured lights and glow sticks. These heighten the hallucinogenic effects of MDMA

- Menthol fumes may indicate the use of MDMA. Menthol is used to enhance the drug effects

Incapacitating Drugs

Door supervisors have an important role to play in protecting male and female customers from drugged alcohol incidents. There are two situations where this can occur. First, the customer may be experimenting with a club drug and may not realise the dangers involved from overdosing or mixing drugs and alcohol. Second, someone may 'spike' a targeted person's drink with a potent incapacitating drug. The same individual will then befriend the person they have drugged in order to move them out of the venue. Once the drugged person is in the 'spikers' domain, they may be subject to sexual assault, rape, physical assault, robbery or murder.

Beating the Spiker

Door supervisors must formulate proactive drills and procedures that make their customers hard targets for any 'spiker'. It is always a good feeling to go home at night knowing that you have cramped the style of some reptile or else saved someone from serious assault. This section will be further sub-divided into six sections.

- Incapacitating Drugs and Rape
- Drug Description
- The Effects of Drugs
- Customer Proactive Behaviour
- Door Supervisor Proactive Behaviour
- Summary

Incapacitating Drugs and Rape

In 2003 the web site at the Women's Rape Crisis Center, Vermont stated that twenty different substances have been used on alleged rape victims. These substances include, club drugs, veterinary drugs, prescription drugs, valium, marijuana, 'downers', sleeping pills, Rohypnol (The Forget-me Pill), GHB (Liquid X), Ketamine (Special K) and finally, the most frequently used drug of all, alcohol. When drugs and alcohol are used in combination, the mix can prove to be lethal. Even on their own, the ingesting of incapacitating drugs can lead to tragic consequences. The effects include, seizures, cardiac and respiratory arrest, coma and death. Check out the web site at Butler County Rape Crisis Program website, (2001) for more information.

Drug Description

There are many good web sites that deal exclusively with the dangers of incapacitating drugs. In order to pursue this subject in more detail, try using the key words, Drug, Rape and Date in your search. The common denominator of these drugs is that they are colourless, odourless and usually have no discernable taste. The spiker will use these drugs in either powder or liquid form. It only takes two seconds to squeeze an eyedropper full of liquid drug into the neck of the target's bottle.

The Effects of Drugs

The effects of incapacitating drugs to look out for are:

- *Drunkenness*. The onset of drunkenness may be rapid. Some of these drugs are 20 times more potent than Valium. The onset can occur within 15 minutes of the drug being administered

- *Sleeping*. The targeted person may fall into a deep sleep. Your best efforts at 'Tactile Stimulation' may fail to rouse the person. Medical assistance will be required

- *Disinhibition*. The reasoning part of the fore brain is the first part of the brain to be anaesthetized by any combination of incapacitating drug and alcohol. The fore brain, when it is in working order, will act as a gatekeeper. It stops the baser impulses from being expressed, either verbally or physically. Incapacitating drugs and alcohol will destroy this control. Because of this fact, the person may appear exuberant, happy and exhibit behaviour patterns that are abnormal for them

- *Vomiting*. Vomiting and nausea are side effects from ingesting Rohypnol, GHB, Ketamine and Alcohol

Customer Proactive Behaviour

Statistics show that you are more likely to be murdered, assaulted or raped by someone you know. In order to avoid adding yourself to these statistics, try the following routines:

- Never loose sight of your drink. From the time of purchase until total consumption, guard it well

- Going to the toilet? Finish your drink first, take your drink with you or discard the drink

- Going for a dance? Allow a trusted friend to look after it, finish your drink first or discard it

- At a social event or party. Bring your own drink, pick up unopened bottles, pour your own and avoid the punch bowl

- Discard any unattended drinks

- Do not accept drinks from strangers

- On the rapid onset of intoxication, nausea or sleepiness, always call or phone a friend, fast

- Constantly check your drink for additives

- Use the buddy - buddy system. Look out for each other at all times. Try not to become separated

Door Supervisor Proactive Behaviour

The following pointers are designed to halt the use of and deal with the effects of Club Drugs and Incapacitating Drugs. These drills are not another set of boring 'Must Dos", they are the key drills that keep all your customers safe;

- Ask the management to display notices that warn customers not to use or supply drugs

- Allow customers to take their drink into the toilets

- Constantly check out the toilets in order to pick up the empty glasses and bottles

- Constantly check the toilets for discarded syringes. If an innocent customer becomes injured, you or the venue owners may be liable for passive negligence

- Constantly check the levels of sobriety of all the customers

- Watch out for unwelcome individuals parking themselves at occupied tables. Go up to the table and ask if everything is OK or else wait until someone leaves the table for whatever reason and you ask them "Is everything OK at your table?" Customers usually appreciate your proactive interest in their safety and enjoyment

- Never allow sleepers or drunks to stay at your venue. Make sure it is a friend, you have identified, that takes them off the venue

- Always confirm the identity of any person who escorts the 'intoxicated' customer off your venue. Enter this information into the Occurrence Book

- Watch any table vacated by customers who have left their drinks unattended. If you have the opportunity, inform them about their security lapse

- Deny access to all known drug dealers or use random searches on the door or keep visual contact with them in order to inhibit their activity. There are also other legal ways that must be used in order to get them out. If you allow drug dealers to operate by remaining passive, the venue will loose it's licence to operate or the victims will sue you

- Use vantage points to scan the whole venue constantly. This will either deny or inhibit illegal activity. You may be addressed at times by customers who say, 'Do you enjoy staring at people, and you have an easy job, nothing better to do?' You are keeping them all alive and safe. There is nothing better than that

- Door supervisors must expect and be prepared to be searched themselves before the start and during their time on duty. An independent person such as the local police force must conduct this search.

Summary

You must reduce your in-house problems by staying proactive and also pre-emptive where necessary. Always try to make the customers hard targets for the reptiles, drug dealers and rapists. A problem created by mixing drugs and alcohol may not be the result of a predator in action but may be self-inflicted. When a suspected club drug situation arises, you must be prepared to treat the situation as a medical emergency and call for medical assistance. If medical assistance is required, place the unconscious person in the recovery position.

Table 5: The Cues for Legal and Illegal Drug Abuse

Legal and Illegal Drugs	Abuse Effects
<u>Depressants and Incapacitating Drugs</u> Barbiturates, Benzodiazepines, Alcohol, Rohypnol, GHB, Ketamine, Club drugs, Veterinary drugs, Prescription drugs, Valium, Marijuana, 'Downers', Sleeping pills.	Lethargy, Sleepiness, leading to unconsciousness Shallow breathing A weak, irregular, or abnormally slow or fast pulse Disinhibition Vomiting Rapid onset of drunkenness Speech problems
<u>Stimulants and Hallucinogens/Rave/Club Drugs</u> Amphetamines, MDMA (Ecstasy), LSD, Cocaine	Excited Talkative Hyperactive Sweating Tremor Hallucinations Over Friendly Overheating
<u>Narcotics</u> Morphine, Heroin	Constricted pupils Sluggish Confused Slow and shallow breathing.

Chapter 7

Intermediate Skills

Use the quiet periods at an event to practice your observational skills and also observe normal crowd behaviour. Select a good vantage point and use it to observe the behaviour patterns of individuals and groups. This time will not be wasted as usually the time you spend will be observing normal, relaxed behaviour. Use the time to observe how the more experienced door staff operate and learn from their behaviour. With time and experience you will soon learn to detect anti-social behaviour developing. This practice will help to develop your observational skills and your roving eye will also inhibit anti-social behaviour.

When you position yourself to observe any crowd, it is your job to spot anything out of the ordinary, long before anyone else. The earlier you spot a problem developing, the much easier it becomes for you to cope with it. Observation involves all your senses. This includes sight, sound and smell. Problems are created when you fail to read the crowd. You have to:

- Know about rival individuals or groups and their relative positions to each other

- Know who has had too much to drink

- Know who has joined company and is unwelcome in that company

- Read body language from a distance. Know the difference between a good-natured argument and a heated debate

- Spot behaviour or activities that contravene the owner's licence

- Spot behaviour or activities that contravene the house rules

- Spot behaviour or activities that others find obscene or frightening

- Spot threats to the safety of bar staff, customers and property. This includes theft, fighting, fires or crowding

Try to avoid extended, direct eye contact when you are observing the customers. If it happens, either move off or pass a friendly comment to disarm the eye-baller, then move off.

If you find it difficult to look at customers, do head counts instead, until you overcome the problem. Counting the customers involves you having to look at each one for a short period, just long enough to deter the troublemaker.

Stay vigilant, pro-active and assertive by continually observing, moving, talking, smiling and thinking one step ahead.

At the start of the night, everyone is relaxed, moving and interacting at a slow pace. The noise levels are low in the early stages of the night. As the night progresses, the crowd will change with the increased alcohol consumption. The volume of the sound increases as the individuals become more relaxed and uninhibited. Verbal and physical abuse will also increase as the evening wears on.

Notice how individuals are using slow body, head and hand movements as they converse with each other and move about. In a noisy bar, when one person is talking the other person is listening by standing side on and tilting their head towards the speaker.

When an argument develops, both people are facing each other, emphasizing the words with fingers stabbing out and their heads are butting forward like two rabid woodpeckers. The antagonists will be moving faster than the normal ambient speed at the venue. They will also go 'full frontal' to each other to increase their intimidating front.

Do not expect all fights to start from a face-to-face position. It is very easy to be caught flat-footed by individuals that enter the venue and make a beeline for their selected victim. These reptiles move faster than normal, bumping into others as they bulldoze their way through the crowd to reach the victim.

Another ploy is for the reptiles to enter the bar and hang about at the counter, waiting for you to move away or the victim to approach. Always challenge suspicious behaviour.

You must always be on the look out for individuals that normally sit with a particular group, but on a specific night, may be sitting away from that group. There are several reasons for this behaviour. First, they may have fallen out with their usual company and are now potential fighters. Second, there may be a fight in the process of starting. By staying away from their normal company, they can ambush any individuals that start a fight with their group.

Keep an eye on the bar staff who may have an abusive or drunken customer in their face. Also make a point of looking at each group of people to see if they have an unwelcome guest in their midst. A subtle facial expression or eye movement is all you need from a pissed off individual to trigger you off in a positive response.

Pay attention to the background noises and this will let you know what is happening at various parts of the venue that you may not have in your visual field. A sudden drop in volume may mean that the crowd has observed something happening and is now focused on that incident. Always head for these areas of silence.

Use your nose to detect wacky baccy, kitchen fires or other obnoxious whiffs. This includes, home made explosives, gas or burning furniture. Never keep your observations to yourself. Always let the other team members know what is bugging you.

Monkey See - Monkey Do

When people in a crowd observe others carrying out illicit acts, and these acts go unchallenged, they are more likely to ape that behaviour. This behaviour has been labelled social contagion (Le Bon G. 1895).

There are many forms of social contagion. Of particular interest to the door supervisor is the contagion of aggressive acts and rule violation. For example, a floorwalker observes a person smoking in a no-smoking zone. The walker fails to remind this person that they are in a no smoking area. You can be sure that within minutes of this behaviour starting, there will be more smokers lighting up, with the situation out of your control.

As soon as a house rule is violated, the crowd must also observe how you are correcting the problem. When illicit behaviour is challenged, it is less likely to be imitated by others.

For example, one of the bar staff approaches you and says, 'I have asked Mr. Buckethead to stop smoking. He ignored me and now others have started smoking and have refused to stop. Can you sort it.' You go to the area and inform everyone that they are in a no smoking zone and they must extinguish their cigarettes. Every other smoker sees this happening and starts to extinguish their cigarettes, long before you reach them. This includes Mr. Buckethead. You go up to him and pat him on the shoulder, with a smile on your face, and the whole group burst out laughing. Another potential confrontation has been averted. It should have been avoided in the first instance by stopping the first smoker from lighting up.

Social contagion also takes place in fighting incidents. When one person lifts a stool or bottle during a fight there is an increased probability that the others involved in the fight will ape this behaviour and escalate the situation.

You must always identify the main players and then attempt to neutralise the threat. Getting the team between the main players and either disarming them or ordering them to wise up and wind down is the best approach. If this does not happen you are now fully committed to a fighting situation. In many incidents where improvised weapons are involved, one or both parties have caused the situation through fear and over reaction.

Your direct intervention can offer protection and cover to the individuals who are behaving out of fear for their own safety. That way, by protecting this type of individual, you stand a better chance of de-escalating the situation.

Team Work and Back Up

To maintain control and good order at your venue, on a permanent basis, you must be skilled in door supervisor teamwork. When all the door supervising staff have a clear role, the whole team will be capable of reacting positively to any incident. The aims of teamwork training and the practical application of that training are to:

- Allow you to present a professional and humane front to the customers and your employer

- End problem situations fast without stressing out the non-participating customers

- Keep you out of jail

- Keep you out of hospital

Meeting These Aims

The tactics used to meet these aims are based on the two basic principles of door and floor work;

1. Mutually support each other always

2. Pre-empt all negative behaviour from whatever source

In all close combat systems you are expected to fight with an interval or reactionary gap between opponents. This safety gap allows the opponents to react to each other's movements. As a door supervisor, you do not have this reactionary gap; you have to communicate with the customers at very close range. For example, the guy at the door is in your face asking why you are denying him access. You are unable to back down, run away or acquiesce to his demands.
Shouting across a crowded dance floor or bar is also out of the question. You must get in close to the ill behaved customer and speak directly to them. This close up approach will give them a chance to calm down without any loss of dignity.
When you are in close and talking, you are vulnerable to attack. It is essential that you always operate with back up, even for low-key routine incident handling. The greater the threat, the larger the back up required. There will be occasions when the back up is insufficient to control the situation. In this scenario, your verbal skills offer a better and perhaps only chance of resolving the situation.

The CCTV Security Cameras

The security video is your friend usually; it will keep you out of jail. When you report to a venue for the first time, always check out the quality of the system as well as each camera's field of view.
Make a sketch of the floor layout and the area outside your venue. After you have completed that task, go around the building again and plot the position of each camera.
Also use the video monitor to confirm this layout and then plot the camera views on the floor layout sketch. The camera angles may not be suitable to meet your operational plans. This includes your assessment of potential trouble spots, ejection routes and all exits.
Make a point of informing the duty manager that you need these cameras repositioned to suit your security risk assessment. There is no use arguing it out in court after the event when you are accused of

assault. A simple adjustment of a security camera well before the event would have supported your statement.

Dragging a bum off camera to sort them out looks just like that on camera. It will prove more productive to stay in shot or back off into shot when you expect it to go ballistic.

It is better to interact in front of a security camera with those involved in anti-social behaviour. This can and will be used if allegations are made against you.

Use the video records to get even. You are not a punch bag for drunken bums. After a ballistic situation, get yourself to hospital to record and repair any personal injuries. Then report the incident through legal channels. Rest assured the bums are also doing that. Expect to go to the police station at any time. You will have to make statements as either a victim, a witness or as an alleged assaulter. Hopefully, an honest statement will be supported by the security video.

Risk Assessment (S.W.A.T.)

The emotional turmoil experienced in stressful situations will disrupt your tactical thinking. Sometimes you may review a rash decision made in the heat of the moment from either a hospital bed or a jail cell.

Risk assessment is the dynamic process of identifying; assessing and then reacting properly to all the incidents you face as a door supervisor. Screw up on this task and your life or freedom will be in jeopardy. Never enter a situation without first, assessing it and then second, assessing your ability to resolve the situation.

Violent situations have a life of their own which is very unpredictable. For example, when you jump into an affray to break up the fighters, the crowd has at least options. First, they may move away from the fight to make your job easier. Second, they may obstruct your approach to the fight and then join in the fight to kick you lifeless.

There are four steps to Risk Assessment;

1. Identify the risk, well in advance

2. Inform the full team of the threat. That is, if you are part of a team

3. Pre-empt and defuse the situation to reduce the risk

4. React positively when the situation goes ballistic

As you walk around the floor of the venue, you must be constantly assessing the mood and disposition of the crowd so that all incidents, when they occur, do not come as a surprise. The practical consideration of the following four factors will help you to assess your situation and then help you to formulate the appropriate course of action. These four factors are:

Strength **W**eapons **A**im **T**errain (SWAT)

Strength

- Do you have someone good enough to cover your back while you try to resolve the situation?

- Is the opposition either physically weak or strong? This may influence the strength of your physical response

- Will you work as a team to resolve the problem as fast as possible?

- Sometimes there are two different groups to contend with, two sets of friends of the two antagonists

- Are these two well-bonded groups that may resort to a group attack if you intervene?

- Are there any leaders or sensible people within the group/groups who will take charge of the situation?

- How drunk are the antagonists? More drink makes people easier to unbalance but they will have a higher pain threshold and behave more unpredictably

- The strength of your physical response must be reasonable and effective enough to neutralise the fighting

Weapons

- The bar must keep the empty bottles and glasses to a minimum
- You must not, and your back up must not possess anything resembling a weapon
- If the fists are flying, are there any bottles, knives or spikes in their hands?
- Your body weapons used in attack and counter attack must not exceed reasonable and effective force

Aim

- Your primary aim always is survival. Never walk into your death, injury or incarceration
- Your secondary aim is to escalate your force to dominate the force used by the opposition
- Your tertiary aim is to resort to instrumental violence before you are too physically tired to control the threat
- Your aim always is the protection of yourself, staff, customers and property with reasonable and effective force
- Resolve or remove the problem subject as fast as possible

Terrain

- Where are the nearest exits to the incident?
- How will the doors open? Outwards or inwards?
- Do the doors have a solid side panel decorated similarly to the door? You can get jammed here on the take away
- Is the take away route clear of slip and trip hazards, crowds and bar debris?

- Having a bad day at the office? Use the walls to jamb punchers against. This reduces the impact of their punches because they are unable draw their fists back

Triggers

A trigger is any form of customer behaviour that demands a response from you. It is impossible to learn door work from the printed page. The printed page is only, at best, an aide memoir for practical instruction or personal experience on a specific subject. The preceding, and mind numbing, checklists are difficult to remember and apply, but with experience, you will become competent at applying all these pointers. Until you can do this, you are simply bluffing your way.
Always try to stay focused on your specific task and remain emotionally active. That way, your tasking acts as a trigger for your behaviour.
When you watch and work the crowd, you are pre-empting their negative behaviour with your own behaviour. Your correct use of body language, dress, demeanour and other forms of social interaction with the crowd is very influential.
On some occasions, your pre-emptive and pro-active behaviour may not prevent negative behaviour from surfacing in the crowd. Here, the customer's behaviour will trigger a response from you. For example, you may observe the slow, casual friendly interaction of the customers changing to a jerky and reptilian interaction. This would trigger off your immediate intervention.
Another trigger would be created when someone leaves their seat or leaves the venue. You immediately check out the area they vacated for lost or suspicious items.
There is one other occasion when you are on a hair trigger. That is when you are trying to cope with a potentially violent situation. You are in close contact with a troublesome customer, watching their behaviour and analysing their demeanour. As soon as their behaviour looks like crossing the boundary into violence, you are off like a bullet out of a gun, before it happens. This will be covered in more detail later on.

The Bad and Mad Last Hour

There are two periods of your duty that demand your total vigilance. The first is when you go on duty and establish your presence. This entails weeding out customers who have been at your venue all day and are now totally blitzed, or close to being so. It also entails weeding out under age drinkers and individuals who have been barred from using your venue but the bar staff are too intimidated to order out. Second, you have to be on your toes for the last bad and mad hour before closing.

The laws for licensed premises may vary from country to state, but the generally recognised routine would be as follows:

12:45 am   Last Orders

1:00 am   Bar Closed

1:30 am   Bar cleared of all customers, final security checks

1:45 am   Complete the Occurrence Book

Well before Last Orders are called, some customers will start sinking the drink very fast. This behaviour includes ordering much more drink than they can consume within the stipulated timings. Expect the usual clichés, such as "I've paid for this drink, so I'm going to finish it" (Oh Yeah, Really???) This is also an important part of the evening to watch out for drugged alcohol rape victims being led off the premises to be abused and sexually assaulted. You also have to be terrorist aware and on the look out for people leaving items behind either intentionally or by accident.

With all the bars and venues in your area closing at the same time, there will be an excess of intoxicated young people on the streets at this late hour. Taxi services will be unable to cope with this surge of people. It may take the transport services over two hours to ferry every person home and clear the streets. The more intoxicated people become, the less likely they are to be accepted by the taxi service. Because of these circumstances, they are also more liable to be involved in the statistics of physical violence, criminal damage, rape or robbery.

When violence occurs off your venue, even a couple of paces from the door, your intervention may force you to operate outside your jurisdiction as well as your legal and hospital insurance covers. To add further grief, in panic situations, there is always the danger of you getting accidentally locked out of the premises to face the reptiles on your own. Never step out and never let the rubbish step in. You may think you have earned your money throughout the night, but this last bad and mad hour is where you really earn your daily bread.

Clearing the Venue Area

As a precursor to clearing the venue area, there are any number of tactics that can be used by the bar staff to disrupt the ambience of the venue and encourage the customers to depart on time. For example:

- Turn the house lights up 30 minutes before last call for alcohol.

- Do not serve large measures, jugs or full bottles of wine on the last call.

- Close down parts of the venue so that the staff can clean up.

- Clear the tables of empties

- Stop the in-house entertainment before last call.

The Ideal Attributes

The ideal attributes needed by door supervisors for clearing venues, particularly bars are:

- Assertiveness

- A sense of humour

- Patience

- Quick and witty verbal responses to any customer 'put downs'.

You are now the last members of staff to interact with the customers. You must interact well so that the customers leave your venue with all their 'feel good factors' still maintained about the venue. Always give the customers at least 30 minutes to finish their drinks after the bar stops serving. With a good humoured and persistent approach, this will be achieved. After this 30-minute deadline, the customers and the bar will have exceeded their legal drinking hours.
Every five minutes you must approach individual customers and groups of customers. Draw their attention and let them know that they are on a countdown to finish their drinks. This is a productive and also

a more refined approach when compared to wandering about shouting the odds in general.

Keep changing over the door supervisor as you carry out this task. You will eventually wear down the customers rather than each other. Inexperienced door supervisors can become dispirited and lose their assertiveness if the customers ignore them.
Watch each other as you carry out this demanding task; let individual team members know your feelings if they are too passive.
More intoxicated customers will require a more persistent approach from the team. When a customer appears to ignore your requests to drink up, you must speak to them and elicit a positive response.
Once the deadline is reached, your approach must change. Stop asking the customers to drink up. Inform them that the bar is closed and tell them to make their way to the exits. Start shouting if necessary. They have exceeded their welcome, and the venue is operating in contravention of the liquor laws.
Make sure the doors are covered at this stage. Some customers will not want to part with their electric soup and will try to sneak it off the premises. This can contravene the liquor laws. You may only have a licence to sell liquor for consumption on the premises.
The bottle or glass being taken off the venue may also be used as a weapon or the customer may fall and injure themselves or others with it.

The Occurrence Book

Some venues may not have an Occurrence Book or may simply produce a Page a Day diary with no clear guidelines on how to fill the log in, or what to report or what entries are required.
Always use the Occurrence Book to record the times of any reportable incident. Do this immediately after you have settled that incident.
At this stage your hands will be shaking from the adrenalin dump so that your handwriting will be below standard. You may also feel more like shoving the pen up the reptiles nose. If one of the bar staff is available, ask them to write the short report for you.
When the bar is closed for the night, you can sit down and write a more detailed and legible incident report before you go home.
From experience I have found that the Occurrence Book, or pages from it, can disappear when you need it most. Always keep a copy or some form of personal account that you can produce when the need arises.

The Occurrence Book must record:

- All the names of door supervisors on duty that night
- Times on and off duty
- Maximum numbers of customers in that night
- Reports of any security, safety, or fire equipment problems as well as property and structural damage observed by the door supervisor that require action by the duty bar manager
- Short one line reports on any accidents, violence, access denials, escorts off etc. as they occur.

A more detailed report can be made later that night to include:

- Any found items
- Any items reported lost
- Any confiscated weapons/items/drugs

The Occurrence Book will also include details of individuals who were denied access, including some of the following reasons:

- They were drunk or under the influence of drugs
- Did not conform to the dress code of your venue
- Refused to be searched
- Had a reputation for disruptive or criminal behaviour or are barred
- Were under the legal age
- Were unable to produce a valid proof of age document
- Refused to pay the entrance fee

- Clearly had an attitude problem that would have distressed other customers

- May have caused the venue to exceed the legal crowding limits

The Incident Report

The incident report is a detailed and honest report of any incident that requires reporting while you were on duty. It includes any fights, escorts, ejections, complaints, and damage to property or accidents.

In many instances the videotapes from the security cameras can support this statement. This report must be completed by anyone involved or witness to a reportable incident. It will prove to be much easier to complete the report when the incident is still fresh in your mind. It may be too late or confusing to attempt this the next day after the police approach you with a caution.

Table 7: The Incident Report

The Incident Report
I am… (Your Name) I Was carrying out my duties as… (Your Job) At… (Name of Venue) At… (Time and date) What Happened… (Describe) Type of Incident Who was Involved… (Staff) Who was Involved… (Customers) What they did… Who was Injured? (Staff) Who was Injured? (Customers) What Everyone Did… Who was Injured? (Staff) Who was Injured? (Customers) What Property was Damaged? What was Said by…You… What was Said by… Staff… What was Said by…Customers… What Action You Took… What Assistance/Support/Back Up you used… Who Witnessed the Incident… Your Signature… Copies to You, Duty Bar Manager and Head Supervisor

The Colour Code and Emotional Awareness

After a night on the door a door supervisor will often go home either mentally exhausted, emotionally drained or still hyper tense. This emotional state is created by the emotional roller coaster ride that all door supervisors take on their nightly vigil.

The constant stress of watching, waiting, coping, stopping, challenging, risk assessing, searching and facing down will exact a toll.

This emotional state is best understood by examining my adaptation of the Colour Code Theory used by the Goshinkwai Combat System in the Self Defence Federation, the late Colonel Jeff Cooper, the US Marine Corps and Geoff Thompson.

There are four colours in this theory, each colour representing a different level of emotional awareness. These are White - Yellow - Orange - Red.

Throughout the night, you will be constantly shifting your emotions through this colour code state. Hopefully you will stay out of the White and the Red.

The emotional highs will stay with you for over 90 minutes after your shift ends, so there is a need to wind down. To reiterate from other sections, it is important that you do not transport the emotional baggage from one incident to the next. It is inappropriate to address a genuine complaint with the disposition you needed to cope with Mr. Anus earlier. Likewise, it is inappropriate to address Mr. Anus in the same way as you addressed a minor query earlier.

Table 5: The Colour Code of Emotional Awareness

Colour	The Emotional State	What You are Doing
White	You are switched off, totally oblivious to anything	You are being a total menace to everyone Probably daydreaming, drifting, drugged or drunk You are unable to take in the full picture
Yellow	You have woken up and are now aware of your surroundings	You are carrying out risk assessments on all the situations and reporting all the threats to the team You are both proactive and pre-emptive in your interaction with the customers You are now ready to react positively to any situation
Orange	Your body and mind are keyed up, ready to handle anything	You are unable to run away from the situation so you de-escalate it, if possible All the hormones in your system are starting to fly through your bloodstream You are ready to go to Warp Factor 10
Red	You are at Warp Factor 10	You are now fighting, moving, talking, shifting, de-escalating and covering each other's back You must not run away If you were too slow in getting to the Red state, the antagonists are already there, fighting, spitting and kicking, operating from their Reptile Mindset

Chapter 8

People Profiles

In this chapter I will discuss customer and bar staff profiles and the more common forms of dysfunctional behaviour that door supervisors have to deal with.

What People Bring to the Venue

The worst possible scenario, the customers and staff bring their own drink and drugs to a venue. These are either ingested or hidden on their person. They will also bring their cultural expectations. Drunken individuals may be portrayed in the media as behaving in specific 'laddish' ways. When this behaviour is adopted, the individual expects it to fall under the impregnable defence, 'Drunk as a Skunk'.

Other young drinkers who have spent their under-age drinking years in back streets and derelict houses soon find that their social skills do not transfer well to a decent licensed premises.

When they also bring their intolerance, food allergies, anger, hate, prejudice and weapons to a venue the risk to everyone else multiplies even more. For example, attributing horrifying behaviour to food allergens has been a successful defence in some criminal cases.

Other people from abusive homes or areas of high deprivation may have an aggressive personality. A poorly managed venue gives them an outlet for their aggression. This involves 'The Abuse Excuse'.

The People Defined

Before the illegal and legal drugs, personality traits and prejudices as well as other external factors take their toll and muddy the picture; door supervisors have to control two clearly defined types of people at their venues. First, there are the law-abiding and second, the socially challenged.

The law-abiding are on a continuum from strangers to friends. The socially challenged individual sits on a continuum that includes some bar staff as well as bullies, recidivists, reptiles and the Alpha types.

The common denominator of all the following groups is the fact that they will use a social skill known as 'Psychological Manipulation'. Their main weapon is verbal abuse and they will use it in public and private to humiliate you, increase your anxiety levels and make you screw up.

Strangers and Friends

The law-abiding strangers and your friends are out to relax in a safe environment but your friends may also be out to see what concessions they can extract from you.

When you are working on the door, other door staff will be depending on you to carry out your duties in an impartial manner. Your support must lie with the team you are working with and not your friends.

Other than abusive bar managers and security managers the worst enemy you can have while working the door are;

- Your friends

- Neighbours

- Off duty bar staff

- Off duty door staff

These people either know you or know everything there is to know about your job. After a couple of drinks, they will not be backward in telling you just what they think of you and how well you are not doing your job. If you turn a blind eye to their activities, such as allowing them to be boisterous or allowing them to stay on for ten extra minutes after last call, you will build up for yourself a whole mess of doggy do.

When friends, off duty bar staff or off duty door staff start to mess around at your venue, sort the problem out without any fear or favour.

If you start moving the boundaries of acceptable behaviour, you start to loose control of the venue. Let there be no concessions - *No Surrender - Keep Control.*

The Recidivist

The persistent offender has spent enough time in prison to learn how to manipulate the unwary and exploit individual weaknesses. Because they have used these black arts on other experienced prisoners and prison staff, ordinary mortals do not stand a chance. As with the dysfunctional alpha type and the psychopath, they will bully, lie to, assault and then put the blame on the person they victimise.
At your venue they will exploit emergency situations to carry out illegal activities. These situations may be created by their accomplices or else be genuine. For example, if someone creates a scene during a search, there is a high probability that others are carrying something and the distraction allows them to pass you by without a search.

By engaging you in conversation they can seek out your weaknesses. Conversation is often used to divert you from moving to particular areas of the bar where their accomplices are conducting illegal activity.

Bar Staff

The bar staff may be off duty from another location or even on duty at your venue. They claim to know your limitations better than you do and will remind you of that fact with monotonous regularity.
Multi-national public houses have one personnel factor in common. All too often they will promote their personnel to their own level of incompetence. In the public bar setting, bar staff can embark on development training programmes and be elected to the ambiguous post of duty bar manager on the strength of a good tick test result.
In some bars such promoted staff do not have the emotional or professional maturity to be in command of customers and staff. If you are the victim of bar managers or duty bar managers who are using inappropriate language or behaviour to abuse and bully you, speak up immediately.
For door supervisors the most insidious bullies and abusers are bar managers of all sexes. This is because door staff will be more unlikely to respond assertively or aggressively to this dysfunctional group in public. As a result the targeted individual goes on to suffer the long-term effects of verbal abuse. It will eventually damage their self-image.
This abuse can produce an individual who is incapable of carrying out his or her duties in a professional and impartial manner. Abusive people understand this process. When they are placed in positions of authority, they capitalise on their authority until their victims are forced

to move away or challenge them. Start keeping a record of abusive behaviour. Use a diary where incidents can be written down and counter-signed by witnesses. Also use a Dictaphone-type recorder when a diary would prove to be impractical.

The key assertive openers to consider in this situation, while your recorder is switched on, are;

- Do you have a problem relating to me?

- I find your attitude towards me offensive, why are you like that?

- We do not appear to have a good working relationship, why is that?

This ploy did not work in the last bar I worked. It had a culture of bias against door staff from the incompetent bar manager on down the feeding chain. For example, the bar manager mentioned on more than one occasion, 'I would trust the word of the bar staff before the word of the door staff.'

Without the support of the Security Manager the job became impossible and all the door staff left for other employment. I remained to the bitter end because the job was such a rich source of material on dysfunctional management.

The bitter end came one night when the door staff were assaulted by a mob and the bar manager left the door staff on the door with blood dripping from their wounds. In the security video tape, shown in court two years later, the bar manager was observed scuttling from the scene holding his head like a Congo chimp. He had resigned one week after the incident and was not available for the court case.

The Bully

Bullies are individuals who have failed to come to terms with their personal limitations. This negative perception of their own limitations can lead bullies to act aggressively towards others. That way they hope to increase their own status and self-esteem. Sometimes the bully has a focus on a specific group and their aggression is expressed through ageism, sexual harassment, racism, or verbal abuse, to name but a few.

Bullies have been portrayed as loud-mouthed wife beating braggarts. In reality, some bullies can intimidate with the stroke of the pen, others quote obscure rules, and others will be very patronising and explain to the victim in great detail how to do a simple job. Others will allow dangerous incidents to occur, simply by an act of omission.

The Victim. There are all forms of victim, such as the new kid on the block, the more popular or more competent, the weak and vulnerable or the beginner.
The new kid on the block may be perceived as a threat therefore the bully subjects that person to a sustained psychological assault. This can spill over to a direct or indirect physical assault whenever the opportunity presents itself.
The victim can also be a beginner or else a weak and vulnerable person. In either case, this gives the bully an opportunity to exercise their superiority at the expense of their victim.

The Tactics. Bullying tactics are used to either dominate the victim, force them to leave the bully's domain or make them overreact and be sacked. Members of the public often use bullying tactics. What differentiates the bully from the public is the way a bully focuses on a victim and persists in their attacks. On a daily basis the bully lies to, goads, humiliates, frightens, intimidates, demeans, belittles and criticises the victim.
The bullying tactics take two forms, Passive and Active bullying.

Active Bullying. For example, the bar manager, staff or a regular customer may constantly criticise your decisions and actions in coping with 'problem customers'. The following classic phrase springs to mind, 'For f***s sake, you are f***ing stupid. Do you not know how to do a simple thing like that'?' If you are conforming to a humane protocol in these actions then you will have nothing to fear.

Passive Bullying. Anything that restricts your ability to do your job properly is classed as passive bullying. If the bar management fails to keep you informed about company policy until it all goes wrong, then they are guilty of using a bullying tactic. Perhaps they will not tell you the legal crowd capacity of the bar, have no continuation training or may fail to support you after a traumatic incident.
How many times has the bar manager 'forgotten' to recharge the batteries on your security equipment between shifts? When you become isolated on the floor or door without proper communications you are the victim of passive bullying. The bully has engineered the situation so that you can be subject to physical assault.

Dealing With the Bully. Never allow yourself to be goaded into using threats or foul language when you address the bully. Everything they say or do is designed to have you removed from your post.

All bullies are past masters with threats. They have spent their life using threats on their children, partners, parents and other victims before you came into their domain. They will have a ready answer every time or use your threat to have you dismissed.

Always challenge bullying behaviour by questioning every criticism, put down and allegation the bully makes. The bully has low self-esteem and a weak personality. A challenging and assertive response to any form of bullying behaviour will force them to retreat.

Alpha Types

The alpha type refers to the successful leaders in society and business. These are important people who have reached the top of the 'pecking order' in their domain.

The alpha types 'lead from the front.' They are the first into the battle, always courageous, tenacious and inspiring. They always give their best effort and expect those under their command to follow suit.

There is absolutely no problem with normal alpha types in society; they create progress and profit. The problem is, 'on the door' you are more likely to meet the dysfunctional alpha, those who are incapable of listening to others or sticking to the house rules. That group includes the gang leaders, drug dealers and paramilitaries. These alpha types live outside the social norms. They use violence, bullying, intimidation and lying to achieve their objectives. It is either their way or no way.

You have a serious problem. In my case I asked the individual to leave before the police arrived. I explained how he had infringed the house rules in front of the cameras and the bar manager did not want him on the premises.

Reptiles

Most people engage in social interaction, drinking and the use of illegal drugs to unwind and enjoy themselves. But, on many occasions, these three factors can produce a monster. Social interaction, drink and illegal drugs will create altered states of consciousness that have a direct effect on the fore brain. This part of the brain is responsible for all aspects of learning, judgement, the regulation of behaviour (Scarf 1976 p. 87) as well as speech control. When excessive drugs, drink or hormones disable the fore brain there is a high probability that rational control through the fore brain will be lost.

Without this rational control, more primitive parts of the brain have a more direct input into human behaviour. Social constraints, empathy, conscience and learned behaviour patterns are forgotten and the individual will appear to behave like a reptile.

The Triune Theory One possible source for the evil and dangerous behaviour exhibited by human beings can be found in the concept that has been labelled 'The Triune Theory'. A concept first proposed by P.D. McLean in 1949 (1973 and 1990). He noted that the human brain is clearly divided into three layers, the Reptile Brain, the Limbic System and the Cortex.

The three sections of the human brain in Diagram 3 represent the major evolutionary stages in its development. This concept is also called micro genesis. Although these three sections are separate, many nerve fibres or neural connections interconnect them.

Diagram 3: The Triune Theory

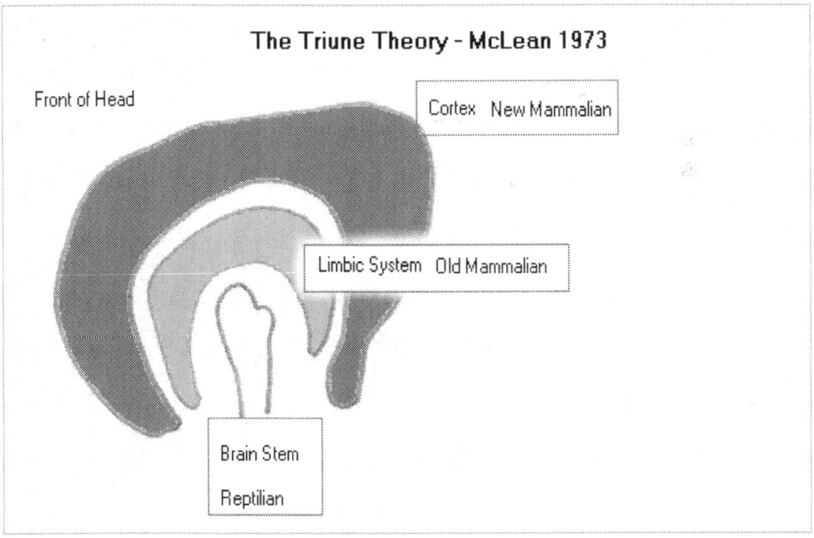

The Triune Theory - McLean 1973

Front of Head

Cortex   New Mammalian

Limbic System   Old Mammalian

Brain Stem
Reptilian

The Reptile Brain. Until now, the Triune theory has not been proven, or disproved for that matter. It is used here to serve as a metaphor, a simple plausible description for the workings of the human brain and an explanation for the horrifying behaviour that door supervisors have to cope with on a nightly basis.

Once you recognise the cues outlined in the following sections for an individual descending into evil and dangerous behaviour, you will be able to pre-empt that behaviour.

Later on, the legal eagles, can dress up their clients, comb their hair and then cite the 'Twinkie Syndrome', 'Drunk as a Skunk' or 'The Abuse Excuse', but when the problem is in your face, you are faced with a reptile.

The Reptile Brain - Responsible for Mechanical Behaviour The Reptile Brain is also called the Primitive or Archipallium Brain is the original brain. It has not changed much over the past 240 million years. This section includes the brain stem, comprising of the mid brain, pons and medulla as well as the cerebellum. From within the brain stem, information from the outside world is relayed to the other two sections of the brain.

The brain stem is responsible for mechanical and instinctive human behaviour. This includes the life sustaining reflex processes of breathing, sleeping and the heart beat as well as aggression, flight, mating and self preservation.

When this part of the brain is responsible for human behaviour, it is expressed as sex without love, including rape and child abuse, road rage, murder and wife beating. There are no signs here that the heart rules the mind or the mind rules the heart, there is only mindless behaviour.

Although it is claimed that there are simple learned responses stored in the brain stem (Ornstein & Carstensen, 1991 p. 96), this part of the brain is incapable of learning from past mistakes.

The Limbic System - Responsible for Emotional Behaviour The Limbic System or Old Mammalian Brain, which surrounds the brain stem, is named after the mammals that replaced the reptiles. The limbic system is the second layer of the human brain. It evolved over 60 million years ago. The main role of this section of the brain is to maintain homoeostasis throughout the body. This means it regulates body temperatures, blood pressure, heart rate and blood sugar levels. Without this process of homoeostasis the human body would remain cold - blooded and reptilian.

The Limbic system also governs the emotional instincts and emotional behaviours expressed in relation to the four F's. These are, Feeding, Fighting, Fleeing and Finally, sexual union. Here the heart overrules the reasoning mind. For example, affairs of the heart, hunches, intuition, gut feelings and instincts can influence an individual's final decision.

At the most basic level, this part of the brain determines how you feel and how you manage a stressful situation. That is, either positive or negative, good or bad and finally, avoiding pain and repeating pleasure.

The Neocortex - Responsible for Rational Behaviour   The grey matter of the Neocortex (Latin for new bark) or cortex is also known as the New Mammalian Brain. It envelops the Reptile Brain and the Limbic System. This third layer evolved over the last million years. Although all animals have a cortex, it is more developed in human beings, comprising of up to five sixths of the total brain mass. The cortex, in evolutionary terms, has been through an explosive development (Hunt 1982 p. 28-30).

Table 8: Cortex Development

Time Scale in Years (BC)	Volume in C.C.s
20 Million	Similar to Monkeys
3 Million	500
500,000	900-1300
200,000-300,000	1400
40,000	1500

The cortex governs reasoning and language. (Eysenck H & M 1994 p. 230) This part of the brain is also responsible for controlling the basic instincts and reflexes of the Reptile Brain and controlling the emotional behaviour created by the Limbic System.

Brain and Behaviour Because of the similarity between the older sections of the human brain and that of fish, reptiles and early mammals, it has been inferred that there are also similarities in behaviour patterns. For example, Susan Greenfield (1997) infers that the Triune Theory might;

'help us understand the literally mindless and uniform behaviour of masses at political rallies.' (p. 13)

As Ardly (1970) states;
'The mob reverts to the Reptilian Brain.'

Koestler (1976) states;

"psychological problems can be traced back to the dysfunction between the three brains."

Montagu (1975) argues against these views. He states that because of the similarities between the brains of reptiles and humans, it does not necessarily follow that there will be similarities in behaviour.

What Montagu has not tried to explain is what happens when the cortex loses primary control and behaviour is dependant on the direct influence of the Old Mammalian and Reptilian brains. This can take place when the individual ingests either drugs or drink or else loses emotional control. Legal terms such as, in 'the heat of the moment,' 'crimes of passion' etc. can be used to account for behaviour brought on by moments of terror or panic.

Behavioural Cues The next chart lists some cues for an immanent fight or Reptilian behaviour. It is imperative that you recognise these cues. This chart simplifies the behaviour pattern of the Child Abuser, the Wife Beater and the Bully.

The individual you are observing is descending into a dark and dangerous frame of mind. They are just about ready to move from the verbal stage to the physical stage of their abusive behaviour. Having already decided to attack you, it is just a question of time before their body floods with adrenalin and they launch that attack.

Armed with the following information it may be possible for you to pull them back from their descent. If that fails you can react positively to their behaviour.

When an individual enters these final stages, you are faced with an individual who has no conscience and no rational control. Their body may be locked solid in bilateral symmetry. In this condition, restraints or any other attempt to move them will fail. You will feel like you are dealing with a solid wall.

This person will then go on to behave like a psychopath. By that, I mean they will act impulsively and recklessly, without a care for the consequences of their actions. If you witness this behaviour pattern it is usually happening, as you are being assaulted and murdered by drunks, drug addicts or enraged individuals.

Dealing With Reptiles Other than using the pre-emptive strike, there are two other weapons you can try that may draw the individual back from their descent into reptilian behaviour. Those are Posture and Verbal Interaction. If you can keep the individual engaged in conversation, while presenting an inoffensive demeanour, there is less likelihood of them going totally reptilian. For example, on one occasion I stopped an individual from fighting by keeping both my palms open, facing him and asked him. "What has happened? What is wrong?" By meeting immanent violence with a concerned attitude and a non-violent posture, I defused the situation and the individual walked off. My palms open stance was non-confrontational but I was one hundred percent ready to dodge away and then whack the bum if his shoulders as much as twitched.

Table 9: The Reptilian Brain is now in Charge

The sentences have become shorter, perhaps only grunts or silence
Their body is hunched forward and locking out, they are almost ready to fight
There are beads of sweat on their foreheads
They are shaking from the adrenal surging through their body
Their breathing is shallow and fast
Their stabbing fingers turn into fists.
Their skin turns from the *red* for the Limbic *rage* to the *white* for the Reptile *fight*
They are glancing away and then glancing back at you to see if you are distracted
They 'Lock Out', in bilateral symmetry. Their body is solid and unmovable
Their faces go deadpan; they are staring, expressionless and about to attack

The Drunken Person

Many of the people that door supervisors come into contact with will be 'under the influence' of drink, illegal drugs, prescription drugs or a combination of all three. At many venues you will be in a situation where young people are experimenting with all forms of legal and illegal substances. The side effects of experimenting with alcohol include 'throwing up', fighting and irrational behaviour.

You can reduce your workload by ensuring that there are no under-age drinkers in your venue at any time and by keeping a more vigilant watch on the younger drinkers. All degrees of drunkenness are dangerous conditions, not only for you but also for everyone else.

Consider this table of statistics from the Health Promotion Agency (NI, 2002), where alcohol has been estimated to be a factor. The important point to note from these figures is that there are more sober people out there committing these interpersonal crimes and your ability to interact with sober people is just as important.

- 25% of roads deaths
- 30% of drowning accidents
- 30% of murders
- 33% of accidents in the home
- 39% of deaths in fires
- 40% of incidents of domestic violence
- 44% of theft charges
- 45% of wounding and assault cases
- 88% of criminal damage arrests

The Long Term Drinker

When a new bar opens in any town or city, amongst the first customers will be individuals banned from all the other local bars. This group of drinkers are, by the World Health Organization's definition, either excessive drinkers or chronic alcoholics. They have uncontrollable drinking habits and a resulting deterioration in basic social skills.
Eventually, they will misbehave and become barred from your venue. Until that happens, you will have to understand the drunken customer and learn how to cope with them. To that end, this is a short psychological/sociological study of the 'down and out' drunken person.

The Initial Approach Drinking in public places and public drunkenness is a common problem in most societies. It is also a problem, which many local authorities have failed to address adequately; therefore this study sets out to understand one side of the problem, the alcoholics themselves.

My hometown has three identifiable groups of public drinkers. The group I approached consisted of a maximum of five individuals at any one time, this included a female. This group had established a regular routine and, most important of all, the group's physical debility through their drinking habits and their inoffensive demeanour, guaranteed my physical security.
It took about one hour for me to gain the trust of the leader of the group; after all public drinking was an illegal act. As soon as my identity was confirmed I made my research aims clear. After that I was allowed to stay and observe for the remainder of the two-hour drinking session. For the next five weeks, I dropped in on the group for at least two hours on a daily basis to note their behaviour patterns. These visits appeared to be random but they were designed to give me an overview of their complete daily and weekly routine from 9:30 in the morning until 11:30 in the evening. I gained further insight into the group on some occasions by simply approaching a lone member of the group and asking him where the group was. By using this tactic regularly, I learned more about the activities and whereabouts of other group members.
It was impossible to become directly involved with this group. Not only was it an illegal activity, it was also unhealthy to drink from the same bottle as individuals with a wide variety of medical problems. It was later noted that any outsiders joining this group for a drinking session usually had their own bottle and refused to share it with or accept

anything from the group. From this observation, it is obvious I was dealing directly with drinkers who had reached the absolute pits. Formerly they had decent jobs and stable marriages, until their drinking became a major problem.

Each drinking session did follow a set pattern, so it did become easier to spot new information and confirm older observations. This information was logged immediately after each session.

The Morning Session Drinking sessions were held in the back alleys, which were close to the most frequently used off licence. They also used the parks because of the seclusion offered by the trees. In the evenings or when it was raining, they used derelict buildings and their own houses.

From Monday to Saturday, the group had a daily routine that never varied. At 9:30 am the group start to meet up in the centre of the town. They are usually very reticent and suffering from varying degrees of Delirium Tremens.

The morning is spent begging and borrowing enough money to buy the first bottles, either cider or wine. By 11:00 am the first purchase has been made and the group move to the drinking areas for the first session. The topics of conversation are centred on TV programmes, soccer, boxing, sex, food, financial problems and the occasional joke. These subjects are discussed, with no deep insight shown by any person.

The Rituals There is an established ritual to the drinking routine. First, the bottle is opened and is passed round the group, who are standing in a circle. The conversation cross cuts the passage of the bottle. After one round of the bottle, it is set on the ground in the centre of the circle until any member picks it up for a second round. A five-member group will have consumed two cans of beer, one bottle of wine and one bottle of cider between them in the two-hour drinking session.

The session always starts off with nondescript chat, which becomes more enlivened as the session goes on, but then it slows down near the end of the session. The beer and cider are usually mixed. The normal procedure is for the individual with the steadiest hands to carry out this duty. The same individual is also employed to roll the cigarettes. This is accomplished from the kneeling position; the individual rests his elbows on his thighs for extra stability. The tobacco is normally obtained by clearing out ashtrays and picking up all butts/stubs/stogies from the ground.

During the sessions, the members urinate within sight of the bottle but defecate out of sight. The defecation points are noted for their puddles of excrement. This is caused by their gastric stomach conditions and liquid diet. At no time did I ever see used toilet paper. The other most notable physical problems are the scarring, cuts and abrasions to the upper portion of their faces. Striking their foreheads and cheeks during their numerous falls while intoxicated causes this.

The Afternoon Session The afternoon session starts at 3:00 pm and lasts for two hours. After that the group breaks up. One chronic alcoholic stays in the town centre until 11:00 pm and the remainder return home. There is no advantage to be gained by staying in the town centre with no one to beg or borrow from.

On Sundays, the group has an alternative routine. This is because there is no one to beg or borrow from in the town centre. Most of the group clean themselves up and visit their relatives for Sunday dinner, some cash and a bag of groceries to help them through the coming week.

Financial Resources The exception to their daily routine of the 11:00 pm start occurs when one of the group members receives their government cheque. On that occasion the drinking starts at 9:30 pm, after the cheque is cashed at the local off licence. The drink purchased with this cheque is shared among the group members.

By 11:30 am this session is over and the group is off again begging and borrowing to finance the 3:00 pm session.

There is a large discrepancy between the fortnightly government cheque and the six-fold amount they spend on drink each fortnight. Further observations noted that this is made up through begging and borrowing on a daily basis. All their available cash goes on the purchase of alcohol. Food is supplied by friends or else stolen. On one occasion, an individual had to run past a supermarket entrance because earlier he had stolen his weekly supply of bread.

Another member of the group had been banned from entering the local chemists because he would, on a bad day, stand and drink the aftershave. On one occasion they berated me for buying them cigarette tobacco. I was informed that their source of tobacco was from picked up butts/stogies and dustbins. My money should have been spent on alcohol.

Psychological/Sociological Interpretation Reciprocity, or sharing, was their most salient ritual observed in this study, in both the procuring and the consumption of drink. I confirmed this reciprocity on one occasion. I presented two members with a can of beer each. One can was opened and shared and the other can was pocketed for future

sharing. Inextricably linked to this ritual is the goal, which is drinking. After each session, all behaviour is directed to obtaining more drink.
I did get beyond the blind acceptance of their idealised delusion of reciprocity and noted that, on many occasions this ideal was breached.

On some occasions the government cheques were cashed but half the money was held back for personal use. On another occasion, the individual did not surface until he had spent all the cash on himself. No sanctions were enforced for this lapse because the culprit is still a future source of revenue.

All participants were capable of articulating their understanding and perception of how the public perceived them, e.g., 'A bunch of drunks', but they always emphasise that although they are aware of how they are perceived, they are unable to stop drinking.
There is a need in complex society for "regularity, precision, individual responsibility and integration through self-control and cooperation" (Bacon 1970). The subculture in this study has demonstrated that most of these values can be perverted for the procurement and sharing of alcohol.

The social structure of this group appears to be similar to the Skid Row subculture described by Rubington (1962), who referred to the "bottle gang relationship". He found that a social relationship existed and was based on easy access to the group. It was the procuring, sharing and drinking from the same bottle, which governed the bottle gang's conduct.

Most towns are caught in a spiral of deviance amplification, with "Drinking Prohibited" notices appearing regularly where the bottle gangs congregate. Future studies into public drinking and drunkenness would benefit if the views of local politicians were included, especially their views on the Seattle study by Spradley (1970). That study has shown the ineffectiveness of criminalizing public drunkenness and the benefits of detoxification programmes.

Eight years after this study one of the group had committed suicide by hanging himself, the woman and two men had died from alcohol related illnesses and one male had reformed.

Long-Term Drinking and Health Problems When you are faced with the long-term drinker, you are faced with an individual who has the high probability of suffering from a multitude of both physical and mental disorders. The long-term drinker may be suffering from any of the following conditions (HPA NI 2002):

- Damage to the liver, heart, brain and stomach.

- Cancer to the mouth, liver, throat and stomach.

- Blood Pressure

- Mental disorders

Serious consideration must me made before using any form of physical contact with older customers who have the potential for these conditions. The door supervisor who goes in too heavy handed and physically abuses this type of drunken customer is liable to face a murder charge.

Dealing with all forms of drunkenness is covered in the final chapter.

Chapter 9

Verbal Conflict Management

I define verbal conflict management as the group of procedures used to deescalate and manage situations where the door supervisor and others are engaged in a verbal dispute. But, despite all efforts on the part of door supervisors, there will always be occasions where these skills fail to work or are inappropriate, inadequate or impossible to implement.

The procedures outlined in this chapter are a humane alternative to a violent response when facing dysfunctional customers. The efficacy of the response of course depends on the type of customer you are dealing with. An angry or confrontational customer with a genuine grievance will prove to be much easier to handle than someone who is deliberately trying to provoke you. The bully, the fighter, the drunken customer, the drugged customer, the off duty bar staff and the manipulator will not respond positively to verbal conflict management procedures. Their aim will always be to provoke and humiliate you whereas the angry or confrontational customer can be placated through the use of verbal conflict management procedures that address and resolve the complaint.

The Three Stages

There are three stages in the process of verbal conflict management.

1. Identifying the type of verbal conflict

2. Selecting the response

3. Reinforcing the response

The Three Constraints

The implementation of any response is always constrained by three overriding factors.

1. There is a need to protect others from stress and violence. Start negotiating in a quiet spot if this is possible and leave the escape route clear for the angry or confrontational customer

2. There is a need for speedy resolutions. There are always limits on the amount of time you can spend on any problem. Set those limits early and have a game plan that works when the deadline is reached

3. There is a need to maintain the venues 'feel good' factors.

Identifying the Verbal Conflict

The door supervisor has to categorize and then manage at least three types of verbal conflict. These categories are,

1. Complaining customers

2. Rule breakers

3. Customers who are arguing between themselves

Selecting the Response

Once the verbal conflict has been identified it becomes much easier to select the ideal response and then implement that response.
There are two general responses to verbal conflict, the intrusive response and the personal response.

The Intrusive Response

The intrusive response takes place when the door supervisor has to intervene between two individuals who are embroiled in a heated discussion. In this intervention the door supervisor will use assertive arbitration. This is because in many cases the door supervisor will end the confrontation by imposing a solution rather than acting as a mediator between the arguing customers.

The Personal Response

The personal response takes place when the door supervisor has to negotiate with an individual or group of individuals. As examples, on the floor the supervisor has to address an individual who has infringed the house rules. The style used in this response is called assertive negotiation. This makes the response more problematic than the other responses. Examples of assertive negotiation are used throughout the book starting with the competing response referred to in The Thomas-Kilmann Conflict Mode Instrument, (Tuxedo NY: Xicom, 1974), also known as the TKI model.

The door supervisor will also have to deal with genuine complaints from irate customers who expect a specific problem to be resolved to their satisfaction. In this situation the door supervisor can use a more flexible form of negotiation. Flexible negotiation places a high demand on the diplomatic and negotiating skills of the door supervisor. In that respect is an ideal response to customer complaints.

The TKI Model This model offers five specific responses to verbal conflict that can be applied in any venue situation. This model is a questionnaire used to determine personal conflict handling responses. It operates on the principle that there are five different responses to conflict and individuals have a propensity to use one form of response to all forms of conflict.

The model recognises that conflicts are best addressed by applying the appropriate response, not the personal choice. This rule is particularly true for door supervisors.
If you have a preference for using one particular response, you may be unaware of the other responses and their efficacy. A good working knowledge of the TKI model will allow you to make a more informed choice when you have to manage verbal conflict.

The five basic responses from the TKI model are Competing, Accommodation, Avoiding, Collaborating and Compromising.

Competing This is an assertive and uncooperative response. I have found it to be the best practical response in assertive negotiations where the enforcement of the house rules or the maintenance of customer safety is involved. The response has to be used when you are faced with people who are exploiting the four remaining responses.

The competing response can be made more positive by using your assertive body language and voice. The competing response involves the use of terms such as, 'We are unable to admit you. The jeans do not meet our dress code.'

Accommodating This response involves the use of phrases such as, 'I will do as you have asked'. It involves yielding to another person's wishes or points of view and sacrificing your own. This response can be used if you make a mistake or come to see the other person's point of view. Accommodation and the next three responses are inappropriate for use on the door or on the floor if the house rules are infringed. But, it can be used when you have the opportunity to be more flexible, such as responding to complaints, when the rule breakers can be cautioned or when customers are arguing.

Avoiding Avoiding an issue involving security and customer safety is entirely wrong. Problems that require your full attention must be addressed. Every problem you avoid can only escalate or be repeated by others who witness your avoiding response to bad behaviour.

Collaborating This is a response where you try to find common ground between the opposing groups. Solutions are usually achieved when the needs and concerns of both groups are met. Again, there are limits, the door supervisor can never collaborate by stating 'You can keep your drugs but don't use them in here'.

Compromising This is a response that partially satisfies both groups through an exchange of concessions. It involves the use of terms, such as, 'I'm only prepared to allow you in if you take off that offensive t-shirt and leave it with me'.

Reinforcing the Response

The verbal and physical reinforcements used in verbal conflict management are designed to enhance your response and resolve the conflict. At the earliest opportunity let everyone know they are on a deadline to resolve their problem. This will speed up the process.

On different occasions, experienced street fighters have walked away from me saying, 'You've done this before'. On some of these occasions door staff have asked me, 'What did he mean'?

Most of what I did in those confrontations was verbal and physical in that I used my voice and body language to win the confrontation and also block every set up the belligerent customer tried to make.

Bold Fear

Always approach the verbal conflict situation with the mnemonic 'BOLD FEAR' in mind,

> **B**lade, **O**pen, **L**isten, **D**istance
> **F**ace, **E**ye, **A**ss, **R**elax

Blading the Body

'Blading' the body is the first move. Never stand square on when interacting with a potential troublemaker. By pointing one of your shoulders and standing half turned away from the troublemaker you appear less confrontational and at the same time you are protecting all your vital mid body targets. Street fighters will realize what you have done and will immediately be more cautious. The bladed body is an obstacle to the street fighter.

Open Palms

Closed fists are a sign of tension, stress, fear and a willingness to fight. The closed fist also represents assault and any good magistrate will fine you the equivalent of one weeks pay for the display, no problem.

Open palms are used as a sign of non-aggression. By keeping your hands open and using them expressively you can keep yourself calm and stop the problem from escalating. You are not just trying to keep yourself calm; you are also calming down the angry customer.
When you use your hands expressively they should be held above waist level in front of your body. Again this represents an obstacle to the street fighter who knows he has a difficult job getting past them before he can do any damage.

Listening Skills

Listening skills are important in verbal conflict management. The listening skills also involve,

- Body language

- Questioning

- Voice.

Body Language In 1967, Mehrabian et al published the results of a series of experiments on what influenced a listener most as to the real feelings of a speaker. He then went on to claim that the speaker's body language had more bearing on communicating feelings.

In 1999 Oestreich refuted this conclusion. He referred to the work of Argyle et al (1970) which shows that when all the verbal clues and body language are consistent with each other the message is much more powerful. For example, angry people send out a powerful message. What makes this message powerful is this consistency between their body language, the tone of their voice and the words used. So, to make your message much more powerful, make the tone of your voice, the words used and the body language support each other. When there is a lack of consistency between these three elements the customer will view this as a weakness in your presentation and will become more difficult to control.

Questioning The worst opening statement you can make is, 'Calm down and stop shouting'. That is equivalent to saying, 'Shut your f***ing mouth you dick head, nobody wants to hear what you have to say'. The reason they are shouting and excitable is usually because nobody is listening to them and they want to be listened to.

Start by finding out the names of those involved and address them by name. Identifying individuals and addressing them by their name helps to destroy their anonymity and thus reduces the threat.

Another poor approach is to use closed questions or orders that demand a simple yes or no response. Using the closed question will never improve the situation.

When you first approach an angry customer always ask them what made them angry. This lets them know you are aware of their anger and want to talk. Always ask questions that start with either what, where, how, who or when. By using open questions like that you will force the angry customer to shift their attention to you and articulate their anger. That tactic usually helps to dissolve their anger.

Voice. If you can stalk close to the angry person, shout as close to their ear 'What is the problem here', but only shout out the first word and then slow down and soften your voice. The initial shout is used to induce a startle reflex. Once you have their attention the slow, quiet words should start the calming process.

When the person starts talking to you, show them some respect and build up an empathy with them by nodding, using 'Yes, yes' or 'I see, I see', 'mmmm', 'ah ha', 'Let me see if I understand' and always repeat some of the key words used by the angry person at the appropriate stages of the interaction.

Distance

When people are interacting there are conventional distances they maintain between each other such as Reaction Gaps, Personal Space and Intimate Space. Comfortable social distancing is difficult to employ in a crowded and noisy bar.

The Reaction Gap   Most combat takes place in situations where a reaction gap is maintained between the combatants. The reaction gap allows you to keep the opponent at a distance. That, in turn, allows you to detect his attack and then react positively to that attack. Customers will feel more comfortable in a stranger's presence when there is a reaction gap between them.

Personal Space   Another important distance is your personal space, that is, when you are close enough to reach out and touch each other.

Intimate Space   Because of the noise and crowding you are usually interacting within each other's personal space. This is known as the intimate space. To the customer's consternation, this distance is too close for a stranger and they will feel threatened. If the customer decides to attack instead of talking you will get hit. To reduce this threat, always use the bladed stance, open palms and keep asking open questions. This will help you to appear more non-threatening to a frightened customer.

Movement   If a person is trying to set you up and you blade your body, they will start to move around you, just keep bladed and keep the door covered. In some situations this can mean stepping in close to the individual. Sometimes you will find yourself confronted by dirty dancers. These are the one-shot wonder boys intent on getting one good hit. They are hopping about and trying to line you up. Screw them up by staying close or moving back. That will ruin their chance to hit and run.

Verbal Distance   Also distance yourself verbally by introducing the third party, the house rules. That way you remove yourself from the centre stage in a verbal conflict. The door supervisor must not operate from a personal machismo mindset but from a mindset that is focused on applying the house rules and maintaining the safety of all customers.
If the customer has a problem, it is with the house rules and not the person enforcing those rules. That way, the process of negotiation should start rather than a man-to-man confrontation.
Always use the 'We' word to show that you are not engaged in a man-to-man confrontation and you have back up. For example, 'We will have to ask you to leave if that behaviour is repeated'.

Switching   Sometimes it is better to totally distance yourself from the problem by switching. If a stalemate takes place in the negotiations, always ask for the intervention of other door staff or managers and then move out of the picture. Also try the Bad Guy routine by moving out of the negotiation and allowing the Bad Guy to do the talking. Then return as the Good Guy and offer the person a 'get out clause'.

Face Saving

Face saving is an important aspect of interaction in any conversation. It is so easy to create fear and insult, reject or embarrass an individual. For example, never interrupt the customer when they are speaking or look at your watch. You must do everything in your power to stop the negotiation from deteriorating into a confrontation.

The potential conflict situation is easier to resolve if you can induce the customer to move away from their friends before you explain the situation or listen to their side of the problem. Most people are reasonable and will respect the opportunity to resolve a problem without losing face in front of their friends.

If the person has infringed a house rule, never criticise them but draw their attention to the behaviour that infringed the house rules, that gives them a third party to negotiate with.

If the rule infringement warrants it, always say, 'That was your final warning, behave or go home'. If they have any sense they will accept the offer and even apologise for their lapse in good behaviour. But, if you say to the individual, 'That behaviour was out of order and these people are upset'. The individual now has the opportunity to say either, 'I do apologise', or 'F*** them', just take it from there.

Face also refers to your facial expression during interaction. You must try not to express your fear, hate, disinterest, anger or disgust. Always focus on expressing an interest in what the other person is saying.

Eye Contact

Eye contact involves looking into someone's eyes occasionally during a normal conversation. This can be used to express your interest in what the other person is saying or to emphasise what you are saying. Avoid staring into a customer's eyes for more than those eight seconds. After that, shift your eyes to another part of their face or body. They will detect any shift in your gaze and capitalise on that shift. For that reason always keep the person you are talking to within view. That way you will detect any imperceptible movements. If you have trouble knowing what normal eye contact is, spend some of your time observing other customers in normal conversation and watch their eye contact.

As soon as you become engaged in a conversation make sure you blink first, blink early and blink often. That way you have eliminated a confrontational element of the negotiation and relaxed the person you are talking to.
When the belligerent customer glances away for a few seconds and then looks back, they are playing Monkey See Monkey Do. In conflict situations people operate at very basic levels and are inclined to copy the opposition. If you punch, they will punch. If you kick, they will kick. If they look away, you will look away and get hit.

Always look at the problem customer and keep looking at the problem customer. Do not stare into their eyes, just fleeting glances now and then or pauses of eight seconds and no more than that. A street fighter will stare you out and when you blink too long or avert your eyes from them you will get hit.

Assertiveness

The professional door supervisor needs to cultivate assertive behaviour patterns. Assertiveness involves looking and behaving like a winner who can pre-empt anti-social behaviour and still be approachable to the majority at your venue, the law abiding.
It also involves letting others know how you feel and implementing the house rules in the face of strong opposition. Assertive behaviour can be learned through observing other experienced door supervisors in action or by timely corrections from the head supervisor on your conduct.

Assertiveness can also be enhanced during training by engaging in role-playing events that emulate the scenarios you encounter at any venue. It also develops when you learn to adopt the following assertive behaviours while you are negotiating, arbitrating and interacting:

- Dress well
- Speak clearly
- Show a working knowledge
- Remain consistent and honest
- Remain firm but understanding
- Remain relaxed and always looking up
- Listen to the customer and understand their feelings
- Have clear objectives of your own and explain them

In verbal conflict management situations assertiveness is the best mindset to use for managing the conflict, expressing your objectives and letting everyone know that there is a time limit to the argument. This deadline is the secret weapon that ticks away. You must keep them aware of it because you will have to take over. You will take the final decision in the matter and they have five minutes to sort their problem out.

Relaxed Body

A relaxed body reflects a relaxed mind and this will help the person you are addressing to relax as well. You will experience fear and stress as a door supervisor and you have to learn to cope. If your mind is disturbed this will be expressed by your uncontrollable bodily functions. Fear and stress will make you shake, defecate, urinate, laugh and cry hysterically or even faint. Hopefully you or your friends will never express these symptoms.

There are other minor symptoms of fear and stress. These include fast breathing, clenched fists, hunched shoulders, the grimace of fear, twirling fingers, biting your finger nails, the stabbing finger as you loose it, fast and high pitched talking, chewing gum like a maniac and the following two guarded poses, The Hitler Pose and The Self Comfort Pose. Once the belligerent or manipulative customer observes these symptoms they will exploit you.

Learning to relax the body and cope is as simple as learning how to inhale and exhale. The following chapter will focus on the fears most door supervisors have to address and then conclude with a process called the Fourfold Breath that will prove to be more beneficial to you than a bottle of vodka.

Diagram 3: Summary of Verbal Conflict Management

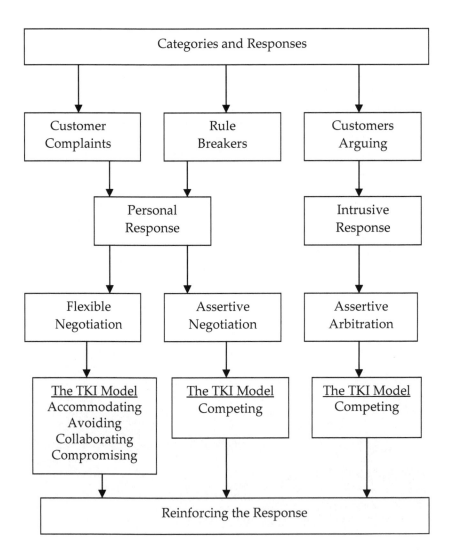

Chapter 10

Stress, Fear and Violence

Door staff have a demanding task and must learn to cope with their emotional turmoil on a nightly basis. This chapter will outline the main factors involved in that emotional turmoil, including stress, fear and anxiety. These and other subjects will then be discussed in relation to violence on the door. The close of the chapter will outline a coping process.

Emotion

The word emotion is derived from a Latin word meaning to move or agitate. It is a word used to describe the inner feelings of the individual under stress. For example, grief, rage, anger, happiness, joy, frustration, anxiety, and fear are all emotional responses to stress.
Behaviours exhibited because of these emotions may be very similar and thus difficult to label. This is because all human beings are uniquely different and it is impossible to accurately predict or measure individual inner feelings. Each individual will respond emotionally in a different way in any given situation.

Stress

> 'I woke up this morning, that was my first mistake' (Anon)

Reber (1985) states that stress is 'a state of psychological tension'. This tension is a result of the mental and physical demands placed on an individual and their perceived ability to cope with these demands. Individual personal skills and experience usually dictate how that individual reacts to stressors.
For some individuals, getting out of bed in the morning is a major stressor, only to be followed by more stressors as the day goes on.
There are two forms of stressor, Mental and Physical. Both forms have been listed in the following table.

Table 10: Summary of The Mental and Physical Stressors

Mental and Physical Stressors Faced by Door Supervisors	
Mental Stressors	Physical Stressors
Insufficiently briefed	Weather conditions
Insufficient training	Under/Over dressed
Too much information to handle	Strobe lighting
Difficult decisions	Loud noises
Dealing with threats and abuse	Smoky/Dark venues
Constantly assessing the risks	Energy sapping restraints
Fighting boredom	Physical/Mental exhaustion
Dealing with problems	Working on after a fight
Pre-empting dangerous situations	No Food/Water/Rest breaks

The Physical Stressors

The physical stressors listed in the table above are anything in the environment that makes the door supervisor feel uncomfortable. Physical stressors will cause physical stress and then go on to cause mental stress. The physical and mental stressors feed off each other in a vicious accelerating spiral of negative responses.

The Mental Stressors

The mental stressors listed in the table above are created by the bar and security management, the customers and by your ability to cope. The mental stressors will cause immediate mental stress and then physical stress such as stomach cramps, sweating, rapid breathing and vomiting.

Positive Responses to Stress

The news is not all bad. Stress can also have a positive effect on human behaviour. Because all stressors can affect you both mentally and physically, if you prepare both your body and mind to cope with the stressors, your reactions will be more positive.

Stress will accelerate your thinking processes; this is a good reason why you should not eliminate fear. The accelerated thinking can result in you making the correct decision in a dangerous situation. When the stress is too intense you will make poor decisions.

When your basic and continuation training involves the use of reality based scenarios, your reactions on the job will have a much higher probability of being positive. Here you follow the correct procedures, identify the threat and respond within a legal framework that keeps you safe.

If you are confronted by a frightening situation that you have not prepared for, there is a high probability that your response will be negative. That is, you either over react or fail to initiate behaviour that would reduce the threat.

Despite the best training in the world, there will be occasions where you totally 'lose the plot'. Fear, anxiety, physical and mental exhaustion will cause you to make a bad decision.

Fear

Fear is one of the human emotions. It is easier to understand when it is accepted as mental and physical distress in response to a specific threat. Thinking about the possible problem areas and all the real dangers creates this distress. Mental and physical distress then creates tension, a nervous energy that is very difficult and sometimes impossible to control.

Fear Defined

The 'science' of psychology has yet to explain how you experience fear. As always, psychology is much more successful at cataloguing and describing our general reactions to dangerous situations and then speculating about the way we process our individual responses to fear. It is not clear to the psychologists if fear is:

- A physical reaction, without thinking, to the immediate danger in front of you

- Thinking about your physical reactions induces an emotional response to the immediate danger in front of you

- A mixture of both the above

The Four Elements of Fear

In 1995, Rosenhan and Seligman described fear by splitting it into four elements. Because fear is such an intense personal experience, it does not follow that these elements, or responses to fear, can be expressed in a predictable manner. The same type of incident can have different effects on the same individual on different occasions. An individual who backs you up on one occasion cannot be depended upon in a similar occasion.

- Mental
- Emotional
- Physical
- Behavioural

The following examples explain these four elements of fear in more detail from the door supervisor's perspective.

Mental   Something happens on the door and you think, "I'm going to get hurt here." The resulting spurt of fear will induce you to make a quick positive response. If there is too much fear you will be unable to think rationally, you will either freeze or over react. This element also includes, worry, confusion, poor concentration and feeling ill.

Physical   The emotion of fear will cause your body to change, both internally and externally. In some instances these changes will occur instantly and you may be unaware of the change.
This includes, the shakes, weak legs, rapid breathing, dry mouth, sweating and awareness of your rapid heartbeat. In order to get rid of

excess baggage for the flight, you may vomit, or experience the desire to urinate/instant urination or the desire to crap/instant bowel evacuation.

Emotional   You experience feelings of dread, terror or butterflies in your stomach. Consider the following scenario. You report in for work at 8 pm. and the first thing the bar manager says to you is, "Hello, there are three guys in here drinking since midday. They were barred three months ago for fighting and they refuse to leave, sort it out". If you don't need a change of underpants after this greeting you are not normal.

Behavioural   The behavioural factors include fight, flight or freeze. You may talk rapidly, chew gum like a maniac, bite your nails, and tap your feet, yawn, and twitch.
There are at least six courses of behaviour to follow when you are faced with a frightening scenario and do not have sufficient support to meet the threat or time to wait for the police to arrive.

1. You can shut the door

2. You can predict the problem and leave the scene before it kicks off

3. When the situation goes ballistic, you can leave the scene

4. You can predict the outcome and pre-empt it with a well-placed palm heel

5. You respond to the attack as it occurs and defend yourself

6. The fear is so overwhelming that you freeze, both physically and mentally and take a kicking

Considering the fact that you are a door supervisor with responsibilities to others, are any of these options viable? Only two! (The first and the fourth). Pre-emptive strikes can be interpreted as assault but they are the only viable reaction when you are in fear of your personal safety. Leaving the scene equates with cowardice and finally self defence and freezing are termed passive, a state that will get you killed.
When it comes to dealing with violence, the basic guidelines are usually ambiguous. It is up to the door supervisor to deal with dangerous

situations and then the hospitals and legal systems to deal with the consequences.

At the end of the day, the door supervisors have to stand their ground, take all the verbal crap, talk down the threat and still stand their ground. Rules of Engagement, Pre-emptive Strikes and 'Actions On' drills for different Incidents will be covered in the next book, *Door Supervising: The Physical Skills*.

Fear Experienced On The Door

Fear is good, "it steers you away from danger" (Kalat 1992). To reiterate, thinking about the possible problem areas and all the real dangers creates this distress. Mental and physical distress then creates a psychological tension, a nervous energy that is very difficult and sometimes impossible to control.

For example, before any boxing match, boxers will experience the physical effects of their mental turmoil. The fear of physical pain, humiliation, or losing the fight can induce bowel movements, which increase in frequency.

There can also be incidences of nervous laughter, sick grins, stomach cramps, vomiting, sweating or trembling.

You can also be sure that the customer you are confronting is also experiencing these emotions. Customers who experience fear will hit out in panic. It is up to you to reassure and calm down the customer at all times through your general demeanour and language.

Physical Tension

Paradoxically, this nervous energy is also an essential aid to individual survival. The total control of fear is neither necessary, nor desirable. The nervous energies created by fear will tense up the whole body and prepare it for either the fight or the escape. When the human body is slightly tense, it can respond much faster than a relaxed body.

Physical tension also prepares the body for the impact of the opponent's attack. Simultaneously, fear will increase the individual pain threshold. This allows the body to cope with more trauma than normal. Blood flow to the surface of the skin is reduced. Because of this, bleeding from body wounds is also reduced.

Focused Attention

As well as physical tension, fear will induce mental tension. The combatants will be mentally focused on the source of the problem and will be operating with a limited level of consciousness. Their attention will be directed straight towards the source of the threat. In this state, they will be unable to hear or respond to advice or other stimuli from any source. This state is termed auditory exclusion.

Combatants will also be incapable of changing their game plans when things start to go wrong. They will also be unable to see any activity that takes place outside their direct view.

One indicator of this combination of increased and focused awareness is the fact that the event appears to be taking place in slow motion.

This is how Focused Attention will affect your judgement. Notice how the *solid* side panel looks similar to the open door. While using the fire escape to eject a violent customer it was easy to mistake the panel for the door, honestly, this wasn't an age thing. After slamming the back of the customer's head into the 'door' several times you will begin to think, "Oh dear, the door will not open for me". Long before the sentence is finished, your eight seconds are up and the customer's friends will be on the case and beat the crap out of you.

The 'Solid Door' is on the left

Your practical training programme must also include ways of coping with the limiting mindset of focused attention. Learn to expand your consciousness during training so that you can see and hear much more than the direct threat and become more capable of amending your game plan to cope with the unexpected. When you are dealing with the immediate threat, there may be other threats on the periphery of your conscious awareness that you should be paying attention to.

The Freeze

Normally people talk about 'Fight or Flight' when placed in a stressful situation. But, there is also 'The Freeze.' This can occur when an individual is unable to cope with a frightening experience and remains passive while they are assaulted. There will also be occasions when your back up fails to come to your aid and simply freezes while you take a kicking.

The freeze can also occur when you have accumulated too much knowledge. If you are spoiled for choice in selecting a technique that will extract you from a dangerous situation, there may be a tendency to simply freeze rather than reacting positively. Having a small repertoire of techniques that can be adapted to suit any situation is much easier to utilise than the application of a specific response to a specific attack.

There are also some individuals who are so good-natured and kind that they are totally incapable of resorting to physical violence, even in their own defence. When faced with a violent situation, they are incapable of acting violently in order to protect themselves, so they simply freeze.

Training programmes must be used in order to weed out people who freeze. It will prove lethal to employ someone in potentially dangerous situations if that person shows no potential for reacting positively.

The Adrenaline Trap

Either through fear or anger, people are caught in the Adrenaline Trap. This is because the adrenaline rush will move your body from neutral to Warp Factor Ten in either fight, flight or freeze. With these survival hormones flying through their body, people are rendered incapable of coherent, rational thought.

This is because the more primitive areas of the brain, the Reptile Brain, start to operate in these stressful situations. In this state, their sole intent is to survive the incident. They are prepared to pummel, kick and kill the object they are mentally locked onto. Humanitarianism and rational thought have now disappeared into the 'red mist' of either total rage or fear. These finer traits will only be resurrected later on by their legal representatives and friends who will ask, "What possessed you?"

On several occasions after a rough night, I went home hung up my suit and went to bed to stare at the ceiling for an hour. The next morning, my wife says, 'You were fighting again last night'. How did she know that? It was because I had forgotten to dust off the back of my jacket. While I was standing there coping with Mr Anus the night before, all the toe-rags and scum were kicking and stamping me in the back. I was on just enough adrenalin to cope with Mr Anus humanely and did not feel the slings and arrows of the toe-rags hitting my back.

That is why you should always have back-up when dealing with the Mr Anus types of this world.

The Red Mist of Rage

Take some time out and preview those exploitive TV shows that manipulate the emotions of others until it spills over into the 'red mist' of the Adrenaline Trap. First, the stage is set with nose-to-nose confrontation between couples. Next, the other publicly humiliates one of the individuals. Their emotional response to this humiliation is predictable.

Notice how it is relatively easy to separate the combatants because of their Focused Attention and Adrenaline Trap responses. They are so focused on destroying each other it is safe to come in from the back, or side and separate them with a simple waist lift and turn. With a few tragic exceptions, this 'red mist' is dissipated almost immediately and the combatants can be brought together again to rationalise their problems in a civilized manner.

A well-known tactic used by bar staff that operate without floor supervisors and some police officers, is to allow the initial mad and bad eight seconds of a fistfight to go on. After that, the adrenaline rush drops and the bar staff or police officers can move in to take control of the situation. Reason does return to the mind of the adrenaline-exhausted fighters and they are quite happy to be separated, or even kiss and make up, in some cases.

The task of the door supervisor is to keep the primitive form of Adrenaline Trap behaviour from surfacing in themselves and in others. Legal systems demand a reasonable and minimum amount of force but this demand will not be met if reason is the other piece of baggage to go along with your bowel contents in a stressful situation. Lose the plot and you lose the fight.

The Shakes

Without necessarily experiencing fear, the natural reaction of the body to dangerous situations is the fight-or-flight emergency response (Ornstein & Carstensen 1991). This is achieved through the release of many hormones, including adrenaline. An increase in adrenaline levels will cause an increase in blood flow to the brain and muscles.

This chain of events has the effect of increasing your strength and energy. It is an explosive energy that can cause different parts of the body to shake. The lips, legs, voice, trunk or hands may be affected.

The shakes may have three sources. (Frijda 1989 p. 139 & 153) First, trembling may result from the physical fatigue of tensing up the body in order to absorb physical/verbal abuse. Second, it may be the result of trying to control or suppress the physical activity created by the released energy. Third, it may be the unbridled release of the raw energy in the initial fight or flight response. The third source is supported by Richardson (1978) who stated that the shakes might be a,

> "rapid involuntary muscular reaction" (p.110).

The purpose of the shakes is to warm up the body in preparation for action. Notice how some men have the habit of shuddering at the shoulders after urinating on a cold day. The rapid heat loss through urination will cause this involuntary shudder. It has the same purpose as that induced by fear, to heat up the body.

Your aim in any situation is to channel and manage this raw energy within yourself in order to stop it from peaking. When this energy surges to a peak, without a fight, the shakes will set in and you will be incapable of reacting positively.

You must also physically intervene before the problem customer's energy peaks because they will become impervious to pain or reasoning and get ready to fight. If you are not using the Surging tactic (see Chapter 11), the best counters to this peaked state are to talk down the fight, switch partners or use the Five Minute rule also explained in Chapter 11.

Pressure Point Tactics

Pressure Point tactics and verbal interaction are usually applied as a form of minimum force in order to gain the opposition's compliance. If you are applying pressure point tactics or pain compliance restraints, ensure they are applied for a limited period. A second only in some cases will be sufficient in order to gain control. A longer period will encourage the adrenal dump to take place in the opposition.

As you use physical contact on the opposition, you must also talk to the opposition. The physical contact will cause a rush in adrenalin.

By talking to the individual you will induce fear and flight rather than freeze or fight. When pressure point tactics fail, it is an indicator that an adrenalin dump has taken place in the opposition.

Under these circumstances, you have to change your tactics. Either stop or de-escalate the force you are using, or else escalate the physical force by applying strikes to other pressure points.

Complex Motor Skill Loss

The effects of The Shakes, the Adrenaline Trap and Focused Attention will not only stop rational thought. They also stop the operation of fine motor skills. Complex skills learned in the dojo will not operate when the more primitive areas of the brain are activated during a stressful incident. Instead of constructing three or four stages into one movement, you will be limited to basic sets of moves, one-one or one-two, one-two. For example, countering a punch in the dojo may involve; parry, wrist grab, straight-arm bar and trip.

In reality the primitive mindset will only allow a short immediate response, an instinctive duck and palm heel jab. As a door supervisor you must train so that your fear based responses involve the minimum amount of force and the minimum amount of complexity.

Aggression and Violence

In violent confrontations the main role of the emotional process is to take your body from neutral to Warp Factor 10 in either fight, flight or freeze.

One of the ways this is achieved is by over riding the rational thinking process so that you react by instinct. This is where the fists and expletives start to fly.

Incidentally, this process also helps to keep your legal eagles in Armani suits. If your emotional response to a dangerous situation is too strong, there is one other physical and mental response that will kill you, that is the freeze.

Aggression Defined

Aggression is defined by Reber (1985) as a general term used for "a wide variety of acts that involve attack, hostility, etc." (p. 18).
Baron (1977) further defines aggression as words or actions whose intent is to hurt another.
From these definitions it can be seen that words, facial expression, stance and language can be seen as aggressive. Direct physical attacks can be classed as violence.
All aggressive and violent behaviour usually have an induced or motivational source. These sources include, Altruistic sacrifice, Paternal instinct, Maternal instinct, Hostile intent, Anger release, Instrumental intent, Fear reaction, Drug induced, Alcohol induced, Pathological disposition, Manipulative personality (Psychopath) and Influential

Altruistic, Paternal or Maternal Violence   An individual uses Altruistic, Paternal or Maternal violence in order to protect others.

Anger Release   The most common form of violence you will have to face as a door supervisor will be Anger Release. Denying access, removing customers from a venue, separating an individual from their electric soup or their friends will inevitably evoke Anger Release.

Fear Induced Violence   Fear induced violence can be expressed when you take someone down on their back in order to restrain them. The individual lying on their back, surrounded by 'men in black' will start to kick up, punch, spit and bite at anything coming within range.
If you do have to take someone down to restrain him or her, always try it from his or her rear. Only go as far as getting them in the kneeling position. This procedure will protect you from the fear induced strikes and bites. It may also lower the incidence of the 'death in custody' syndrome and positional asphyxiation, which can occur in the application of face down restraints.

Instrumental Violence   If you have to use violence, let it be instrumental, a controlled aggressive act with a specific goal. The goal will be the compliance of the subject with your demands. This is done to protect you, others or property when all other means have failed or may be inappropriate under the circumstances.

Hostile or Pathological Violence   Hostile or pathological violence is used by individuals who have 'lost the plot' and are intent on punishing someone for the sheer hell of the act. Using this form of violence is both morally and legally wrong. For example:

- After the incident has been neutralised and there is no longer a threat

- Using it to get even with a 'wind up merchant'

An Example of Aggression

A man in the bar verbally insults and then physically attacks his wife by throwing drink at her because she refused to f*** off (*Pathological hatred*). You ask your partner to cover your back while you go forward to rush the perpetrator out the nearest exit (*Instrumental*). After the initial eight second rush, your focused attention causes you to mistake the solid unmovable side panel for the actual door and your grand plan slams to a halt. While you try to open the 'door' with repeated slams of the back of the customer's head into the panel. He starts punching out (*Fear*).

His seven drunken friends all leap in and start attacking you and your back up (*Altruistic, Pathological, Angry, Drunk*). You cover up and jam your two attackers to the wall with your forearms on their throat. This constricts their arm movements and weakens the power of their punches. Their weakened punches are hitting the top of your skull.

After a few seconds you feel the power going out of the punches so you break away and look for your back up. It would be wrong if you choose this moment to hit out at your two attackers. They are now exhausted from their exertions, and because they are no longer in attack mode; your follow up would have to be classed as assault.

You now go to your 'Back Up' who is still being attacked and intervene (*Altruistic, Instrumental*). The attackers all leave the bar before the police arrive. The incident lasted less than one minute.
Eight assholes barred for life from entering the premises and the two door supervisors are labelled hard bastards for facing them in the first place. Incidentally, no matter what label you hang on the violence, all the punches hurt. Overall, that was not a bad outcome for one night.

Anxiety

Throughout this chapter I have discussed fear and the human response to fear. To reiterate, fear is an immediate response to a specific threat. Anxiety is an emotional feeling of dread, anticipation or apprehension that something dangerous *might* happen.
Your response to a fearful incident will make you feel ill, sweat, tremble or knot up your stomach, but only temporarily. Anxiety will make you feel like this *all the time*; in most cases there are no rational reasons for this state. Mild forms of anxiety will promote cautiousness (Kalat 1992).

Coping With Stress, Fear, Anxiety and Violence

Emotional Baggage

There are nights when you have to deal with a whole series of problems. Each problem will have it's own emotional baggage. Always make sure that you do not carry that baggage from one problem to the next. It would be entirely wrong to approach the venue's family table to discuss why the meal was served cold with the attitude you just used to eject Mr Anus for crapping in the emergency exit. For your own sanity and protection it is imperative that you learn to switch to neutral.
It is equally important that you do not carry the emotional baggage from one night to the next. Interacting with customers using last night's bad mindset will only lead to more grief.

Stress, Fear and Anxiety Management

In my approach and experience, there are three aspects to stress, fear and anxiety management. I have called it a management process because it is virtually impossible and undesirable to control any of these conditions in relation to violence.

- First, you do not want to eliminate your immediate response to danger. If anything, you want to sharpen your perceptions of potential dangers. A heightened awareness of the danger will eliminate pain and also help you to respond to and escape from dangerous situations.

- Second, you want to train your body repeatedly in simple one step drills. These drills must be based on countering typical threats you will experience on the job. This way, when the danger presents itself, there is a better opportunity for the learned subconscious behaviour to over ride the body's crude and sometimes legally inappropriate response. Subconscious behaviour? Did you really have to think about a simple drill you carry out without thinking about on a daily basis? It is like driving a vehicle and changing gears, you just do it. It would take thousands of repetitions in order for a physical response to become a subconscious act. But, after a smaller percentage of repetitions something else happens. That response may not become ingrained enough to become a subconscious act. These repetitions will build up a simple closed memory loop in your mind where you can go on to consciously perform the act when required. The memory loop covers muscle memory and knowledge as well as limited experience in the application. That's enough to get you out of an 'O F***!' situation.

- Third, you must learn to anticipate all the dangers facing in your role as a door supervisor. Working on this training programme will not only prepare you for fear responses, it will also inoculate you from the anxieties the job produces.

You may not have the training time that allows you to react to an incident subconsciously. But, the mere fact that you have practised a drill at all means that you are operating in familiar territory. You have an experience to fall back on or adapt in order to deal with the situation.

This response to danger has to be based on realistically tested techniques. If not, your response will be inappropriate and lead to total failure in the real world.

The Fourfold Breath

Just as fast breathing reflects the stress and fear you are experiencing, slow breathing will slow down and calm your thinking.

1. Breathe in through the nose for four seconds, expanding the stomach and then the chest

2. Hold the breath for four seconds

3. Breathe out through the mouth for four seconds

4. Hold that for four seconds, then repeat the process

Before you know it, your hands open, the manic mastication of the chewing gum stops, your shoulders relax and you are ready to walk through the gates of hell into your venue.

Chapter 11

Tips and Tricks

The science of psychology tries to posit that human behaviour can be predicted to occur within a specific time frame and it can also be predicted to follow a specific pattern, within an indeterminate degree of probability of course. As a door supervisor, it is your responsibility to monitor the customers under your charge and predict their behaviour. You are constantly looking for behaviour patterns that can lead to ugly incidents. The quicker you spot these incidents, the faster you can intervene and resolve the problem.

Based on your experience you can predict behaviour within a degree of probability, just like the scientist. For example, when a customer accidentally bumps into another customer, there is a high probability, or a ninety-nine percent chance, that the accident can be resolved without your intervention.

On the other hand, if both customers are drunk, in a crowded and heated environment and drink is spilled, there is a ninety-nine percent chance of an ugly incident developing if you fail to act.

Headache Tablets?

Carry the maximum dosage for 6 hours, enough for yourself. Why? It's 8:30pm ... the first and hopefully the last fracas has been sorted out. When a fracas starts, you can't say "Hold on a minute son while I warm up these old bones." The heady brew of body chemicals will throw your body and mind into Warp Factor 10 in a fraction of a second. When the fracas is over, the body will pay the price.

At 9:30pm the pain starts to kick in. First there is a slight headache from your strained back and shoulder muscles. You then have to soldier on for another 5 hours, coping with the post-traumatic stress and the physical strains. Headache tablets are the best answer to the aches and pains. Anything stronger, such as alcohol or drugs will only dull your senses and interfere with your ability to carry out your duties.

Taxi Phone Numbers

Throughout the night, you will be asked for taxicab numbers. Use a computer to run off a list of numbers, in extra large type. Cut this list into narrow strips for carrying in your jacket pocket. This prevents you having to constantly repeat the numbers to a person who may be slightly drunk and unable to string a couple of digits together. The individual can go on to tap in the numbers at their own pace, leaving you free to do more important things.

Boredom

It is a quiet night, nothing is happening. There is only a small crowd at your venue. You 'switch off' and allow a minor situation to pass without intervening. One second later your whole world goes ballistic and it serves you right. When you relax and 'switch off' you become passive and this allows minor incidents to explode.

Be Pre-emptive and Proactive

It is not good enough for the door supervisors to simply react to situations as they occur. On the door, you must position yourself optimally in order to prevent problems. Never allow anything either in or out of the event that is not allowed to go in or out. Conducting yourself like a winner and moving in before an ugly situation develops is preferable to an ugly scene.

The more pre-emptive and proactive your approach to the job becomes, the less chance there is of a problem either developing or deteriorating.

Bouncer's Eye

There is a very common injury in Sniper Training. This occurs when the soldier forgets to hold the rifle securely enough to stop the recoil from bringing the brass rim of the sniper scope into sharp contact with the eyebrow. The resulting half moon cut was known as 'Sniper's Eye'.

A similar injury can occur in Door Work, if you wear metal-rimmed spectacles. A sucker punch will embed the metal rim into your cheekbone and the bridge of your nose. You can call this condition 'Bouncer's Eye'. There are two solutions to this problem. Either take up a more relaxing past time, such as wrestling with Polar Bears, or else buy spectacles with bevelled plastic frames.

Don't Say It

Actors have hang ups about certain words, even the word Macbeth. Door staff also have hang ups about certain words, such as, 'It's a bit quiet tonight?'

Know Your Enemy

The worst enemies the door supervisor will ever have to face are the incompetent, uncaring and abusive bar managers and security managers.
All too often the door supervisors are at the bottom of the 'feeding chain' when it comes to respect and man management. Some bar managers like to be able to say, 'I've already sacked him', when it goes wrong for the venue.
In many cases the security manager is charging the venue as much as possible for security and paying the door supervisor as little as possible. I always feel that under payment by the security managers is a form of theft. This constant theft breeds a contemptuous attitude in some security managers and that has lead to other abusive practices.

Mind That Door

Another indicator of how individuals feel about you occurs when you open the door and greet customers into your venue. Most of the customers can interact with the door supervisor at this stage, but these are a small section of customers who either ignore you or display an arrogance that entices you to slam the door into the side of their heads.
Some door staff will have difficulty in performing the simple act of opening the door for customers entering their venue. They are not servants and the job is very demeaning for some.
Opening the door for customers is not only good manners that help to establish the feel good factors for the venue. Door opening is symbolic in many ways. For example, it is an act of control because it lets the customer know you are in charge of the door and you are allowing that customer to enter your venue. That way you have established your role from the very start.

Twenty Questions to Die For

There is nothing more frustrating or humiliating than failing to answer a simple question asked by a customer. It becomes a sad reflection on your professionalism and competence when the customer walks away from you shaking their head in disbelief at your total ignorance.

1. Where are the VIP/Councillors/Artiste/Disabled Persons car parks?
2. I represent the local council Health and Safety committee, how many people are in tonight?
3. Where do I get change for my car park ticket?
4. Can my friend bring her wheel chair in here?
5. Where are the toilet facilities for the disabled?
6. Where is the phone?
7. Where is the cigarette machine?
8. Give me the number of the taxi service.
9. Where is the nearest bus stop?
10. How do I get to the main road from here?
11. Where is the drinking water?
12. Where is the first aid post?
13. I'm from the local Health and Safety Committee. What is your role in an emergency evacuation?
14. I'm having an anaphylactic attack where is the nearest hospital?
15. Where are the toilets?
16. What time are last orders?

17. What are the meal times?

18. Why am I barred?

19. Are you qualified to do this job?

20. Me and my six friends with the Mickey Mouse masks and the baseball bats want to know why my friend was thrown out last night

Mystery Guest Check List

Company executive staff, local Council officials and Health and Safety inspectors all expect to be greeted at any venue by staff who have high standards in social skills, dress and behaviour. What follows in this section is a Check List/Report used by a national company specializing in the licensed trade. If you can meet these requirements, you will:

- Establish a good image on the door

- Establish the Feel Good Factor for the venue

- Have an easier time interacting with the customers

The Check List

- Were all the door security staff polite and courteous on arrival?

- Did the door security staff open the door for you?

- Were all the door security staff clean-shaven, with no facial metal or medallions?

- Were all the security staff dressed in the correct uniform?

- Were any of the security staff using personal mobile phones?

- Were any of the security staff consuming drink or food within sight of the customers?

- Were any of the security staff either smoking or chewing gum during your visit?

- Were any friends standing chatting to the security staff for prolonged periods?

- Were any of the security staff behind the bar serving themselves at any time?

- Were the security staff properly distributed, posted and positioned around the venue?

- Were all the security staff responding correctly to incidents?

- Were all the security staff polite and courteous on your departure?

- Final Comments

Catching the Monkeys Performing

At times you will have to speak to a customer who is borderline for ejection. You talk to the individual for a short period in order to resolve the issue without having to eject them. At this stage turn and walk away, but before you take your third pace away, turn round sharply to face the individual again. Every so often you will catch Mr. Anus standing there offering you a one fingered salute or Kung Fu shadow boxing your back. You now have him for bad attitude and abusive behaviour. Guess who's going home early?

Sometimes you will catch someone acting suspiciously. Perhaps they are trying to remove bottles or glasses by hiding these items inside their jackets. Again.... walk away, but turn and look at them before the third pace. If they are going to do something illicit, that's when you catch them out.

Table 11: Lies and Replies

Lies	Replies
I'm the new Bar Manager and you guys can rely on my full support at all times.	Gee, that's great. It's nice to have a good working relationship.
If you let me in big man I will give you a....	No thank you sir, I've just had one.
Do you know who I am?	If you don't know who you are, I'm not letting you in.
Let me in. Let me in. The guy that stole my mobile phone is in there ...let me get it back...I'll only be a minute...I'm the DJ's assistant...I'm the drummer.... I've only just finished checking the bar accounts.... I'll have your f***in job.... let me see the manager. Now!	Conversation's over. Go away.
You are too old for this job.	So?
You are not throwing me out of here!	No sir, I'm only asking you to leave.

Restraints

If you move a subject to the nearest exit and they are conforming, do not stop the momentum in order to reinforce your crude hold with a technical arm lock. Once you stop the momentum, you lose control. If the subject is not actively resisting your escort, keep the subject in that frame of mind for as long as possible.

Arm and wristlocks, in most cases, work through the pain compliance of the subject. Drunk, 'spaced out' and fighting mad individuals will not feel pain. To your total consternation, they are capable of straightening out their arms from holds that have you howling in agony on the practice mat. If you do decide to force an arm lock on that little bit further you will find that pain compliance holds are the rocky road to dislocation, hyperextension, hyper flexion and litigation.

If you do use an arm restraint on a drunken person, use it to simply tidy up the individual without inflicting pain. By that I mean, stop the individual from flapping about, spilling drinks, hitting customers or pulling you off balance. You will appreciate the advantages of this procedure the next time you have to escort Mr Rubberlegs from a crowded bar.

Repetitive Tasks and Brain Fag

Try standing at a door for ten minutes and saying repeatedly, "May I see your pass please?" You soon realise that your mind is switching off. The words have become a mantra that dulls all of your senses.

Learn to carry out the simple task without becoming simple yourself. Head supervisors can help by constantly monitoring and if necessary, rotating the tasks more frequently. You can help yourself by modulating your voice or varying the terminology. Do anything that will break the closed loop of simple task - simple mind.

The same numbing experience will occur in situations where you have to remain static for extended periods. The mind and the body will slow down if they are not being constantly stimulated. A dull mind and body will react much slower than normal. You will also be less articulate when this skill is most required.

It is a constant battle to fight this condition. You must always remain vigilant and capable of responding positively to all threats.

Large Venue Aide Memoir

If the venue you are working at covers a large area, you may need a small sketch of the area. This will help you:

- To locate yourself

- Give assistance to the customers

- Pass accurate messages by radio

- The sketch should contain information on:

    o   The compass points

    o   Main roads

    o   Internal roads

    o   Disabled facilities

    o   Emergency exits

    o   Main entrances

    o   Toilets

    o   First Aid Posts

    o   Fire Points

    o   Information desks

Medical Aide Memoir

The opposite side of the card can be used as an Aide Memo for all call signs, channels and emergency procedures, for example:

- Information Needed To Prepare The Medical Teams

- The exact location of the casualty

- Possible medical condition or physical state of the casualty

- Approximate age of the casualty

- Male or female

Large Venue Radio Procedures/Protocol

Door supervisor, cleaners, bar staff, medics and all other staff must be allocated different channels. This will help to prevent the door supervisor going to Code Red (emotionally) every time the bar staff order Chicken Curry for table 40.

If you have to call the medics, switch to their channel and report the incident. Once you have done this, switch back to your own channel and inform your controller or head supervisor about the situation. This procedure will ensure rapid deployment of the medics as opposed to a second relay of an important message.

If you see any accident, however trivial, report this to the medics, even when the customer appears to be OK. Remember, they could be excited or intoxicated; this will mask their pain until after the event if they have injured their ligaments, tendons or muscles. Furthermore, someone else may fall victim to the same slip or trip hazard.

Immediately after dealing with an accident, consider calling in the maintenance or cleaning staff to sort out the hazard. When you observe an accident and report it, you must complete an accident report for future reference in the event of legal proceedings.

Keep all radio messages short and clear. Ensure that your radio is never on permanent send, blocking out all other radio communications, including emergency messages.

Constantly check that you are on the correct frequency, some radios can be accidentally switched off.

When using your radio, try to eliminate background noise. This will help you to hear and also transmit clearly.

Bribes and Threats

As a doorman you will be subject to all forms of abuse, threat, compliment, insult and inducement on a nightly basis. Take for example an event that is fully booked. Individuals or groups will be desperate to gain entrance into the venue. In fact some groups may try to gate crash the event and you will have to be prepared to close the door on them and call for assistance.

Individuals may offer compliments..."You stupid moron, I hope when I'm 60, I'm not throwing people out of bars.' Others may offer inducements, such as, 'Well big boy, if you let me in you can have anything you want. I will do anything for you'. The women are just as bad, 'Listen muthereffer, let me in or I'll have you knee capped.' It is also very demanding to carry out an impartial job in some cities where the streets have memorials to door staff who refused to comply with the demands of local hoods and drug dealers.

Never abuse your position on the door by accepting inducements of any nature, be they promises, drugs, money, sex or drink. When anything is offered, it is better to refuse politely, without exception. This will protect your professional status. It will also protect all the customers who have legitimately entered the venue and expect high standards in health and safety procedures.

Terms of Endearment

While carrying out their duties, door supervisors are always being verbally and physically abused by the frustrated, drunk and evil people in society. The behaviour, role and characteristics of door supervisor work, in having to deal with this verbal and physical abuse, are sometimes seen as the dispositions and characteristics of the door supervisor themselves.

The following terms of endearment are directed at door supervisors on a nightly basis. Try not to take it personally, be happy. If they are insulting you they are not kicking or spitting, just yet. There may be time enough to talk them down before they go totally 'Reptile'.

- Ole Man River
- We know where you live
- I'll f***in burn you out
- Jerk off
- I saved your ass last week, let me in
- Numb Nuts

- You're f***in easy
- Specky Bastard
- Baldy
- Grandpa
- Fat Shit
- No Dick
- Asshole
- Undertaker
- So you're not fully retired then?
- Is that other bouncer your son?
- Where is your Zimmer frame?
- Too young
- Are you pair for real?
- You should be home with your pipe and slippers in front of the fire

Never take your eyes off or turn your back on the screamer, even when it is a woman. These terms are used as distractions for the opening punch or kick. The Reptiles in their adrenalin pumping up stage also use them. The verbal abuse acts as a courage builder and a first step towards a physical attack. On some occasions you will have these terms of endearment screamed at you by individuals speeding past your venue in their autos.

The list increases with each duty, wearing down the more faint hearted until they eventually screw up. Counter this form of Bear Baiting by mentally noting the number of insults directed at you. That way, it becomes a tedious bore. Any new insults are treated as amusing additions to your mental list. This approach will allow you to adopt a more professional attitude to your job.

Verbal Abuse Has a Purpose

Verbal abuse is the universal trademark of the abuser, the wife beater and the bully. They have an innate drive to dominate and control the situation. In the street or bar scenario, they are screaming in order to pump up on adrenalin, preparing to launch their attack or force you into overreacting. You must use this verbal tirade stage to prepare yourself for the physical assault, perhaps even pre-empting that assault.

Why Am I Not Allowed A F***in Drink??

The core reason for stopping a person's supply of electric soup is your genuine concern for their personal safety. If you work and converse with this non-aggressive principle in mind, there is a better chance that your message will be accepted by the drunken person and their friends.
The more drunken a customer becomes, the more unlikely they are to have access to public transport. They will also provide behavioural problems for their more sober friends and other customers. The drunken person's condition can only deteriorate in the short term, leading to even more behavioural problems. The door supervisor and the bar staff are the first in line for making a decision on the care of the drunk by stopping the supply of electric soup. This is a traumatic experience for some bar staff and they will need your moral and physical support in order to enforce the decision.
If others accompany the drunken person, you or the bar staff may decide to stop drink getting to the whole table. That is, until one person from that table accepts responsibility for the care of the drunken customer and escorts them from your venue and takes them home. After all, it is illegal to serve alcohol to an individual who is in a drunken state.

Educating Bar Staff

Most misunderstandings between the bar staff and the door supervisor can be reduced and cleared up if the Head Supervisor is invited to give short presentations or a question and answer session to bar staff on their training day. A short presentation on the duties and legal limitations of the door supervisor to new bar staff would also pay dividends. The following points must be stressed;

- The bar staff will not give the door supervisor orders. The bar staff can only supply information or ask the door supervisor for assistance

- Experienced door supervisor will always carry out a risk assessment before responding to information from the bar staff

- In the absence of the Duty Bar Manager, altercations between bar staff and customers will place door supervisor in the role of the arbitrator. This is where the door supervisor has to try to de-escalate and then resolve the situation

- Door supervisors will never go physical with a customer who is not going physical with either themselves, door supervisors, others or property

The Progression of Force Model will be explained in the second book in this series. Experienced door supervisors will always allow the customer to leave the bar with their dignity intact. Sometimes this involves the door supervisor allowing them to finish their drink. All this to the consternation of the hysterical bar person involved, who would rather see the door supervisor stick the bottle up the customer's nose.
Door supervisors expect bar staff to complain to the bar manager about the door supervisor's handling of an incident involving a customer who has 'put them down' and wasn't bounced out the door.

Don't Be The Fall Guy

If you wish to retain everything you consider precious, such as your freedom, kneecaps and testicles, think carefully before reacting to demands from bar staff. It is not just the customers who close down their rational mind and behave like reptiles, bar managers and staff are just as guilty. An altercation at the bar can leave bar staff with an emotional high. A successful 'put down' by a customer or a customer who knows he is the victim of a short changing scam will make the slighted bar person look for revenge. Guess who the fall guy is? ... The switched off door supervisor!

Hysterical bar staff demands, such as, 'Get that bum out of here now!' or 'Why is that bum still in here?' must always switch on your survival mode and not Mr. Animal mode.

As a door supervisor on the door and the floor, you are responsible for maintaining security at your venue. You may be dealing with several ongoing situations at once. All demands from whatever source must be prioritised. This means you have a much broader perspective on the floor than the bar staffs' immediate problem. For example, the person causing the problem may have a genuine grievance that demands attention from the bar manager, have good paramilitary, thug or hood connections, have plenty of back up in the bar, be a total nut case or be totally drunk.

As a door supervisor you will stand on your own and go down alone in the bar and the court. Don't expect the hysterical bar staff to back you up, they never will. They have now regained their composure and quite correctly view your plight as self-inflicted.

To reiterate, every time anybody says, "Get that bum out of here!!!".............. say "Why?". If they can articulate a coherent and legitimate reply, then act. The excuse 'I was only obeying orders' is very limp.

Escalating and De-escalating or Surging and Switching

After years on the doors you will experience all forms of verbal and physical attack. This includes threats, punches, kicks and insults. Occasionally you will get lumps in your trousers from a good threat. You remember these moments and on some occasions feel tempted to use these threats and postures yourself. This is because you are always trying to keep trouble away from both the door and the floor without resorting to fighting. Physical fights will ruin the venue's reputation and you will be out of work when the customers stop visiting.

Without resorting to violence, and only using brinkmanship, the veiled threat, numerical or physical dominance, verbal escalation, verbal de-escalation and verbosity you are employing the best tools in the trade. These tools can be used to stop a situation from going ballistic. It is not always advisable for you to escalate a situation in order to resolve it. But you can verbally escalate the situation provided you know when to pull back again and achieve a resolution. This tactic is known as Surging.

You are entering the customer's personal space, giving ultimatums and then withdrawing. After several repetitions of this tactic you will have peaked the customer's adrenalin several times without following up.

You are soon left with a customer who will 'bottle out'. They will be shaking like a leaf and all too ready to talk and walk. Because you are playing out a well-rehearsed drill with several stages it is unlikely your adrenalin will start surging until it is required in the last stage.

Switching over with your partners, several times if necessary, can also unsettle a problem customer. Sometimes a problem customer can focus on one door supervisor or a door supervisor can become too involved in a situation. Irrespective of the circumstances, the head supervisor, yourself or your partner will find a plausible reason for you to be replaced during such an intense exchange.

The problem customer now has to start explaining their case to another member of the door staff. If the customer has to slow down and articulate their problem again there is an increased chance for that problem to be resolved.

This procedure also offers the customer their 'get out' clause, they can blame you, everyone can apologise and the situation can be resolved.

Preventative Measures

As a door supervisor you must always be part of a team. Your chances of becoming a victim of verbal, physical and sexual abuse are reduced when you take the following preventative measures.

- Always operate within visual contact of each other

- Always challenge abusive language from whatever source

- Always operate within a strong supporting team

- Know all your emergency drills and 'Actions to Take' in an incident

- Change the lay out of the bar. For example, alter the seating arrangement, transform a trouble spot into a condiment counter or create family areas

- Install extra internal and external lighting

- Provide personal radios for the staff

- Install surveillance cameras

- Increase the number of floor and door staff

- Increase the bar prices to help eliminate the street trash. The extra money can fund the extra security needed

- Install adequate ventilation systems in order to reduce over heating

- Increase the number of bar staff. This will help to reduce the waiting times (and frustration) and also keep the tables clear

- Use undercover staff with radios or mobile phones to spot drug dealing or other illegal activity that may take place out of sight of the uniformed floor and door staff

- Provide staff training in customer care. This will help to reduce conflict or misunderstandings between staff and customers

- Strictly control the number of customers at your venue. This will help to reduce overcrowding as well as reducing the demands placed on staff

- Your biggest enemy is the incompetent/uncaring/abusive leader. Sort them out fast

Chapter 12

Non-Violent Incident Response Drills

Your primary objective as a door supervisor is to maintain the security and welfare of all the venue customers. You have to learn to prevent trouble, not to deal with it. The more proactive and pre-emptive your behaviour is, the more remote the chance is of trouble starting.

Responsible venue owners have a duty of care for their customers and staff. When you do come into physical contact with a customer, the venue owner should demand a full explanation for your actions. Responsible owners will not take lightly to a door supervisor who is either incapable of preventing trouble or always jumps in, feet first, to sort out a simple altercation. Only resort to physical contact when you honestly believe there is no viable alternative.

There is another good reason for not making a habit of fighting with the customers. It is the fact that you stand a good chance of getting the crap beaten out of yourself. At any one time, most bars will have a handful of resentful customers you have 'spoken to' or sorted out on previous occasions. They are waiting to even the score.

Outlined below are the drills and 'Actions On' for dealing with venue incidents. The common denominators used in every drill include:

- Cover each other's back at all times

- Whenever possible, approach any incidents from behind the antagonists

- Know your drill before you deal with incidents

- Know where all friends and foes are located

- Move in fast and take them out fast

- Resolve the conflict as quickly as possible

Response Drills

A drill is an operational procedure for dealing with a specific situation. Once you have been trained in coping with all the problem scenarios, your general demeanour will be one of confidence. You will take on the persona of a guy (or gal) who has the edge. That is, you will always be in control and dictate the terms in any situation.

Throughout this work, detailed descriptions of specific scenarios have been presented and should be rehearsed. This procedure will help you to cope with the fears and anxieties produced by this dangerous job of door supervising. With practice and experience, you will also become more competent at modifying the basic drill to cope with the chaos of real life situations. Without this revision in real life scenarios, your survival is limited.

In order to promote speed, self-confidence, and fighting skill, the revision sessions must contain as many variables as possible, for example;

- The attack can be structured as a rush attack, rear attack, side attack, group attack, ground attack or combination attack

- The defence can incorporate withdrawal, ground fighting or mutual support

- The opponent can be tall, short, fat, thin, drunk, crazed, sitting, standing, prone or armed. You will be amazed at how impractical some techniques are when you try them on an opponent who does not resemble your training partner in shape, size or demeanour. It can prove lethal for you to experience one of those "Oh F***!" moments in a real situation when a revision session would have eliminated this blind spot in your fighting response

- The conditions must also be varied and represent your working environment. Train within a crowd of people, in a cramped room, in darkness, your hands may be restrained by others or you may be stunned

The Good Guy - Bad Guy Drill

Proper stage management of the roles of Good Guy - Bad Guy will defuse the majority of explosive situations. This routine is a very useful low-key method for dealing with minor arguments, the slightly drunken and barred individuals.

The role you adopt and the tactics you employ will depend on who reaches the incident first as well as the type of incident. The first door supervisor, the Good Guy, goes in talking and the other door supervisor, the Bad Guy, provides the cover. It is up to the Good Guy to either initiate talking or physical action, depending on the incident. It is the role of Bad Guy to stay in the background and act as an unknown quantity, to psyche out the individual.

The Bad Guy must give the Good Guy the confidence to deal with the immediate incident without having to worry about background activity. The immediate task of de-escalating is very demanding. It places you at a disadvantage; you are very vulnerable to attack, not just from the problem customer but also from his friends.

To summarize...

Good Guy

- Talk down/de-escalate the problem

- Befriend or dominate the customer

- Physically control the incident

Bad Guy

- Cover the Good Guy from outside intervention

- Provide physical back up if the incident goes physical

- Psyche out/distract the customer by standing close behind them

Dealing With Lost Mobile Phones

Provided a mobile phone has not been stolen and either switched off or the chip removed to disable it, try the following successful drill:

- Find out what the ringing tone sounds like

- Position the friends of the person who lost the phone in the places visited by the person who lost the phone

- Position the floor staff in areas not covered

- Ask one of the friends with a mobile phone to call the lost number

- Wait, walk and listen for the phone ringing

Dealing with Wet People

Occasionally your vigilance will allow you to spot problems, just in time to catch the problems before anyone becomes embarrassed.
From time to time people who have been drinking can urinate themselves without realizing it has happened. Males wet forward and females usually back, it's all to do with the plumbing.
The best face saving protocol is to approach one of their friends and tell them what has happened. Once you have convinced them you are genuine, tell them to escort the person from the bar.
The best way to preserve their dignity is for them to take an upper garment off, tie the sleeves round their waist and go home.

Dealing With Blood on Your Clothing

It's not the blood you should worry about, but what is in the blood. It may contain drugs, Aids and other STDs, hepatitis and tropical diseases. It might even be someone else's blood. If you have a cut and contaminated blood enters the wound you will be in deep doggy do.
The bloody garment can be steeped in cold salty water and vinegar, before washing. But the fact is, do you have to bring a contaminated item of clothing into your safe home environment? That is something surgeons or doctors will not do. The bloody garment should be treated the same way as contaminated clothing in a hospital is treated, bin it.

Dealing With Groups

When a group of people arrive at your door it is imperative that you do not allow them to intimidate or rush you before you check out:

- Age
- Group identity
- Appropriate dress
- Barred persons
- Disabilities
- General demeanour
- Level of sobriety

By identifying the group you will be able to direct late arrivals to their tables. After they have passed this initial hurdle and you have established your control, you must identify the group leader. You may have to speak directly to the leader of the group at a later stage concerning the behaviour of the group.

Some studies have stressed the point that you must never address individuals within a group. Always address the whole group. Wrong! By addressing individuals within a group you are breaking down the group mentality. Isolate the troublemakers every time and address the troublemakers every time. Destroy the anonymity created by the group and you decrease you problems with the group.
If it is a last night of freedom type of party, the best man or woman may also want the function to go well. This factor will make your job much easier. Stag nights and Hen parties are hard work but less dangerous than sports groups. At this early stage you must inform the group about the house rules, conduct, singing and strippers etc. It is much easier to inform them while they are sober. Trying to enforce the rules after a few rounds will only lead to grief for you.
You are not trying to put the 'mockers' on the function before it starts, a short, sharp and friendly exchange lets the group know that there are limits.

The noisiest group you will ever have to deal with is usually a hen party. High-spirited girls have a high-pitched voice that will penetrate the darkest recesses of the bar. Some bars will not allow hen parties to gain entry for this reason. If your bar does allow hen parties, warn them at the door to be on their best behaviour.

Dealing With Errant Regulars

You can be sure that regulars to your venue will want to remain regulars. At times these regulars may contravene the house rules. Perhaps one night they all sit on, well after the last call. If their behaviour is bad enough, you can caution them on the spot. But, the best time to caution regulars about their errant behaviour is the next time they arrive at your venue. Before they gain admittance, they will be sober and in a rational frame of mind, ready to enjoy themselves. At this stage let them know how unhappy you were about their recent behaviour. Provided they display the correct attitude and response you can allow them into the venue.

Dealing with Sitters

There will be rare occasions when the customers refuse to acknowledge your count down and sit on five minutes after the 'drinking up time' has run out. This has an effect on other customers who see your apparent lack of assertiveness as a chance for them to sit on and enjoy themselves at your expense and the owner's license. Another fine example of monkey see monkey do.
Assertiveness, and lots of it, are required to deal with this situation. Make sure that the bar staff are clear from the area and you have your back up in position. Target one table that refuses to move. This table should be in full view of all the other tables or at least within earshot of what is about to happen.
Half the floor staff act as cover while the other half clears the targeted table of drinks, using thumb pressure point techniques if necessary. The drinks are then poured down the sink. Long before this happens there will be loud wailing and gnashing of teeth from those parted from their electric soup. Control the chaos that follows, letting the other tables know that they are next on the hit list, if they haven't already left.

Dealing With Arguments

A heated, intense argument can lead to physical assault, even when you physically intervene. Your aim in dealing with arguments is to:

- Physically and Verbally Intervene

- Act as a neutral arbitrator

- Suggest a compromise that resolves the argument

First Warning   The best plan for de-escalating a heated argument is for the door supervisors to get close to those arguing. Close enough for them to be aware of the door supervisor's presence. This phase must last no longer than five seconds.

Second Warning   If the initial intervention fails to cool the situation you must verbally intercede. Just a short simple sentence that tells the potential combatants they have an active outsider in their face. "Is everything OK at this table, folks?" Your aim at this stage is to intervene, you may have to listen to both points of view and then suggest a compromise to these points of view.

Final Warning   If the second intervention fails to resolve the problem, warn them for the last time that his or her conduct is unacceptable. Because they are only verbal your intervention is only verbal. If the argument continues, you must *tell* them to leave the venue.
This procedure is designed to stop the antagonists from going physical. You should have helped to disrupt their intense focus on each other by presenting an outside threat. Force the antagonists to acknowledge your presence and respond to your questions. Answering questions demands a rational response, which, in turn, draws the antagonists back from the brink of physical aggression.

Dealing With A Barred Individual

The bar manager draws your attention to the fact that a barred individual is using the bar facilities. Both of the door supervisors approach the individual. The Good Guy gets in his face and the Bad Guy will ideally place himself to the side and slightly behind the individual and also face his friends. This positioning will isolate the individual from his friends and also allow The Good Guy to face these friends as well. The conversation will go something like this...

Good Guy: 'The bar manager has informed me that you are barred. Please drink up and leave the bar.'

Individual: 'No, I want to see the manager.'

Good Guy: 'No, the manager is unable to see you tonight. You must drink up. Come in here tomorrow and speak to the manager personally.'

Individual: 'I want to see the manager.'

Good Guy: 'You are leaving the bar as soon as you finish your drink. You are now trespassing on these premises. You are out of order.'

Individual: 'Why am I barred?'

Good Guy: 'Discuss that with the manager tomorrow. You have five minutes to finish that drink. We are moving back, we will be back in five minutes.'

You move away five or ten meters and eyeball the individual for five minutes. You have left him with no other option but to drink up and leave the premises. Try enjoying a drink with two rottweilers standing ready to rip your arms and legs off. Sure enough within the five minutes the glass is empty. No one else saw anything happening.

The potential major ejection has been averted by making the individual sweat.... he decided to leave with some dignity and the option of talking to the manager the next day.

Please note, if you have been over zealous in the application of the rottweiler tactic the individual can now start legal proceedings to have you charged with causing fear through the threat of violence. Think about that the next time you are on the door with Mr Anus in your face, mouthing off in front of the CCTV and your pocket recorder. If you have legal obligations to meet 'on the door' so has Mr Anus.

How I Used to Win Six Rounds – An Old Style Drill

The following scenario developed because the individual involved in the ejection had a working knowledge of the door. Because of his knowledge he decided to push my patience and good nature to the limit by posturing and ignoring my polite requests for him to leave the venue quietly. This is not a very common problem, as most former and active door supervisors will acquiesce to your requests, respecting the difficult role you have.

I broke the rules and used threats in this situation because of this individual's working knowledge. But, provided you have the numerical strength and the reputation to command the situation, you can overpower troublemakers without having to use open threats or go hands on.

Round One

My back up and myself are asked by the bar manager to approach an individual who appears to have upset one of the female bar staff. The bar staff can be extremely sensitive at times, particularly so when they think they have their own personal rottweilers on standby. You go to the bar counter along with your back up.

I opened the proceedings as politely as possible with, "Excuse me sir, you appear to have upset one of the bar staff with your verbal abuse. The bar staff are refusing to serve you and the bar manager wants you to leave the venue."

First round to me. It's the bar manager who wants the individual off the venue, not you. That way there is no direct confrontation. I am just the messenger. He has caused a breach of the peace by using abusive language and must leave the venue.

Round Two

The Individual. "Are you throwing me out, man?" The individual, an ex-bouncer, folds his arms and towers over you.

You. "No sir, I'm not throwing you out. I am asking you to leave the venue. You are no longer welcome. Come back tomorrow if you want."

Second round to myself. All my remaining teeth are still secure. As well as that, my ears and nose have not been nibbled away. I have verbally dodged the direct confrontation again. The individual has also been introduced to the concept that he is unwelcome and is now a trespasser. As a trespasser still on the property he has caused another breach of the peace and must leave the venue. The individual has not been barred from the venue yet. If he behaves himself he knows that he can come back tomorrow.

Round Three

The Individual said, "I've just paid for this drink and I'm not leaving it."
I replied, "That's OK sir, you can finish your drink. You have five minutes to do that".
Third round to myself. I managed to meet every objection with a de-escalating response. The individual is now on a deadline to leave the venue within the next five minutes. He has taken a verbal battering and a couple of adrenalin surges that took him nowhere. So far and I have not flinched from completing my objective.

Round Four

One of the bar staff says, "Why is that ass hole still in the bar?" I said to the bar manager, "Tell the bar staff to keep their noses out when I'm working on a guy. I'll speak to you later about this."
Round Four to me. Keep your cool and control the incident at your own pace. Your objective is to remove the individual from the venue without anyone going to jail or going to hospital or the other customers being traumatized. Your objective is definitely not based on the hysterical ravings of the 'upset' bar staff.
We are now approaching the stage where the unwelcome guest can still comply with your requests or start to go loopy.

Round Five

After three minutes the individual walked from the bar counter to his table and picks up another bottle to start drinking again.
From my vantage point on the stairs, I give him another adrenalin surge by shouting across the bar, "You still have five minutes and counting!"
The Individual replied, "Don't try that shit on me man!"
I splayed out my hand and shouted again, "Five minutes and counting!"
Two minutes later the individual mutters away to his friends and then leaves the venue.
Round Five to me. Initially I had tried the Mr. Nice Guy approach, prepared to state my case and allow the individual to leave the venue with his dignity intact as possible.

For round five, he pushed his luck so I deliberately escalated the situation. I was prepared to go physical and I let the whole bar know that. All this despite the fact that my scrotum was now so tight my nuts were crushed. I would probably have walked up to the individual with a limp. My cover was just as bad. The protracted incident and the lack of activity had caused his adrenalin to rush and he was shaking like a leaf.

Round Six

I said to the bar manager. "I'm getting rather annoyed by your bar staff interjecting when I'm working on a guy" or words to that effect.
Bar manager replied, "Yes, but they were listening to him when you walked back to your vantage point with your cover. He was saying things like, he will leave in his own good time, nobody was going to throw him out".
I responded to the bar manager, "He was off the premises within five minutes of my initial approach to him. Nobody went to jail, nobody went to hospital and nobody in the bar was traumatized. What's the problem?'
The bar manager could only say, "No problem. That's the way it should be"
Sixth Round to you. Slighted bar staff are inclined to get upset when you refuse to behave like their personal rottweilers by tearing a smart-assed customer apart in front of them.
Door Supervising has now changed to such a degree that Surging is no longer an acceptable tactic because it can lead to a physical confrontation. It could be classed as causing a breach of the peace because you are deliberately causing fear and alarm.
No matter what the outcome I was playing out a drill I had used many times before. In the end I (and my backup, of course) would have gone physical and he knew it. The individual did not want to fight but I did not know that until he walked out the door. The Switching drill would have worked just as well in this situation and it would have been less confrontational. Hindsight is a great instructor.

The Sequel

A couple of nights later when I was off duty, my partner had to face the same individual on his own. He tried the five-minute routine to shift the barred individual. For his pains, the barred individual picked him up in a bear hug, carried all 250lbs of him to the front door, kissed him and went on his merry way.

The Moral of the Story

If the socially challenged know you are operating under-strength they will screw you.

Dealing With Trouble at The Door

When an aggressive customer is standing free with plenty of space to move about in, they have an indeterminate set of options to use against you. Because of this freedom, their behaviour will be too unpredictable. Should they attack, your defensive response will be too slow and you will suffer. Control and dominate the aggressive customer, mentally and physically by standing properly, touching or holding them and talking to them in a specific way that allows you to predict their reactions.

You must always strive to dictate the pace of events and control the potentially violent situation. This can be achieved by:

1. Reducing the options

2. Controlling the space

3. Controlling the dialogue

Reducing the Options

Your stance must at all times, present both a physical and mental barrier to the person you are confronting. Use a side on stance in order to present as small a target as possible. This stance will also reduce the options available to the potential attacker. Your hands must be used to cover your upper body. This in turn will present another obstacle for the potential attacker.

Keep your palms facing the person. This looks more non aggressive and may reduce the tension of the situation. The open palm position will allow you to immediately carry out palm heel attacks, slaps and also parry their fist attacks.

In order to further limit the aggressive customer's options, physically restrain them in a non-aggressive way that will elicit a response from them. For example, the simple act of holding the back of their nearest elbow and pushing it across their body will close down their whole body. This will lead them to committing an act that you have already predicted.

By reducing the aggressive customer's options, you have also reduced your options. This will help to make your response more positive and successful.

Controlling the Space

Show them the threshold, the physical and mental barrier that they must not cross. The point where your personal space starts must be clearly delineated. At the same time you must physically cover the door so that anyone trying to gain entry will have to force his or her way past you.
Keep at least two meters clear behind yourself. When you have to instinctively duck, jump back or shoot back, you will do this without impacting against the wall.
Always try to manoeuvre the other person so that they do not have a solid object, stairs or steps immediately behind them. It is difficult enough to cope with the after effects of 'dropping' someone with a couple of clean shots without having to cope with the blood and concussion from a busted skull.
If you have the time, always close the door on the problem. If you are at a double door, close one side. That way, the opponent will be more vulnerable as they try to gain entrance to your venue. For example, if the door way is narrow they will be unable to use haymaker punches.
The narrowing of their front also restricts their fighting to a couple of minor tactics, such as kicking out to force you back. You are less restricted on the other side of the door. You have more scope to react to the gatecrasher.

Controlling the Dialogue

Fights on the door have a general three-phase pattern.

Phase One. The individual will try to talk their way into the venue. You must explain why they are not allowed into the venue. Always try to stay as impersonal as possible.

Phase Two. The individual will start to pump up on adrenalin, getting ready to rumble. If you do not insult them, they will work on an excuse for attacking you. For example, 'You must think I'm some kind of asshole?? Don't you?' You must keep calm, do not argue but do keep talking. Always try to resolve the situation by using your de-escalation skills.

This is your last chance to defuse the situation. If you have back up, try to step back and allow the back up to replace you. This switching tactic will force the individual to start all over again. It will stop the individual from focusing solely on you. Always let the opposition know that they are fighting more than one person. The situation must never deteriorate into a personal man to man fight.

Phase Three. The situation starts to go physical, you are being tested out and the individual is still pumping up on adrenalin. They are no longer talking, just grunting and growling most of the time. They will push their chests forward to push past you. You push or turn them back.

They have mentally noted your stance and how you reacted to the initial pushes, you are now about to be attacked. They will go silent and wait for you to look away or become distracted. When you take your attention off the Screamers, the Reptiles or the Fighters you will get hit hard.

The confrontation is now approaching physical aggression so shut that door. The follow up to this type of situation will be covered in more detail in my next work, The Physical Skills.

Delaying the Use of Force

Force is the last resort in most situations. There are whole batteries of declarations of intent you can use to curb anti-social behaviour. The majority of people that you approach in any venue are generally co-operative and law-abiding. A polite word and a joke that is not insulting or does not cause any loss of face can resolve most incidents.

The wrong approach to a situation can lead to misunderstandings and an escalation of the problem. This is particularly true when you are dealing with intoxicated individuals. Drunken customers have an innate ability to focus on to a single word in your sentence and turn your quiet approach into a belligerent debate.

Always be prepared to wait a couple of extra minutes in order for the targeted individual to finish off their drink and leave under their own steam. If the targeted person does not present an immediate threat, always take it slowly. That approach will save the reputation of the venue.

When these individuals and the observing customers reflect on how you handled the situation, what will they think? Perhaps they noted you did not insult or hit them. Perhaps all of them will respect that and the errant customer will apologise to you the next time they return.
I always feel good when a customer I respected returns that respect.
Some of the following fifteen approaches will help to resolve a situation without having to go physical;

1. Inform the individual that their behaviour was "Out of order". This will give them something to barter with rather than forcing them straight into a physical confrontation. Draw the person to the side to speak to them rather than humiliating or embarrassing them in front of other customers. Always talk softly, slowly and be assertive at this stage

2. A silent physical presence can sober up the transgressor

3. Increase your numerical strength in the vicinity of the problem

4. Ask the individual to conform to the House Rules

5. Inform them that no more drink will be served to their table

6. Inform them they will be barred in future from the venue if they do not wise up. This gives the individual something to haggle over. If you introduce the physical interaction too soon, it will leave them with no other option but to fight, shout, squeal and struggle

7. Plant the seeds of doubt in their minds. Tell them, "Isn't it time you lot were finishing off?"

8. Stop drink going to that individual

9. Stop drink going to the whole table

10. Have the bar staff clear their table of empty bottles and glasses. This gives the whole table a feeling of impending doom. The more stable individuals will soon talk the others down or walk out first. You also have to clear a route for the 'takeaway' by shifting chairs, tables and innocent customers. This will also

induce 'Impending Doom' and 'Surging' but it is an essential procedure for the health and safety of all customers and staff

11. Use the "I'll be Back" approach. Tell them they have five minutes to sort their lives out and walk out under their own steam. This usually cracks up the hardest bum. Even a bum sitting with a full dose of adrenalin, testosterone and alcohol surging through their system will find it impossible to maintain their belligerence for this extended period. You have closed all escape routes on the bum except the exit. The talking stage is over and their belligerence expires long before the five-minute deadline expires

12. Use the Good Guy/Bad Guy routine

13. Use the bar staff or manager to ask the belligerent to leave. Not only are you acting as back up but also these individuals can act as your eye witnesses if the trouble escalates. Most troublemakers will use this approach to insult the door supervisor. They acquiesce to the requests of the soft target, smirk at you and then walk out. This way, they leave the venue without losing face and even have the opportunity to insult you. Who cares, as long as the bum is off the premises, without a fight? You can catch up on them the next night when they are sober. As they fail to gain admission you can remind them about their misbehaviour

14. Ask them to leave the venue, without escorting them out

15. Tell them to leave the venue by following you out.

Chapter 13

The Drunken Customer

The majority of problems with drunken customers can be attributed to poor judgment on the door and floor, aggressive promotion and irresponsible serving.

Dealing with the drunken customer is like taking part in a stage show, or sometimes it's a pantomime. All the sober customers will be watching your antics as much as the drunken customers to see how well you perform.

If you afford the drunken customer some dignity and a caring attitude you will impress other customers. Perhaps in the old days you impressed the customers with your scruff of the neck and 'wedgee' extractions but those days are long gone.

Health and Hygiene

" Oooh!...It must have been something I ate dear"

Always remember to wash your hands after you have come into physical contact with a drunk before you use the toilet or handle food. This is because some habitual drinkers as described in chapter 8 are noted for their filthy clothing, the occasional vomiting session, poor hygiene habits and the persistent need to shake hands with anybody they can focus on.

I do not think I'm being too paranoid or pernickety on this issue because during my health and hygiene training I viewed material on the transfer of bacteria and germs from contaminated to clean surfaces and immediately related this to my study of the habitual drunk. By washing your hands occasionally and always before using the toilet or handling food you will stop transmitting what was on the habitual drunk's dick, hands, nose, mouth or ass to your own dick, nose, mouth or ass.

Dealing with the Bar Fly

As a door supervisor you will be confronted by individuals suffering from all the different levels of intoxication and dependence on alcohol. At a new venue that has not weeded out all the obvious drunks and troublemakers, you will have to recognise the more subtle activities of those who have escaped the immediate banning. Some of their moves are obvious, such as going to the toilet and returning with a glass of beer stolen from another table.

The lone alcoholic will usually seat or stand themselves either close to the venue entrance, where there is a high volume of customers walking past or at the bar where customers have to buy their drink. From these positions he/she is ideally situated to either greet or bid farewell to all the customers. This is the first stage of begging for drink. They will remain in position all night with some beer in their glass until they trap a sucker for a drink. Some customers are so expertly conned or drunk, they do not realize they have parted with their hard earned cash.

It is only when the individual becomes a pest through persistent begging that they have to be escorted off the premises. In some cases, individuals are quite successful at this art and you will fail to detect them for weeks.

Identifying Drunken Customers

Your first task when you go on duty is to go through the bar and identify under age drinkers, drunks and barred individuals, who all have to be removed. Always try to identify the degree of intoxication of all customers at your venue and then get them off the premises before they become a danger. Do this by asking the bar staff which customers have been at the venue the longest and then look for the visual cues.

There are several reasons for identifying drunken customers as soon as you go on duty. For example, drunken customers will only become even more so. They also represent a liability to the health and safety of not only themselves but to anyone else in their vicinity.

Assessing Drunkenness

Degrees of intoxication are difficult to gauge because drunkenness is relative to:

- Body weight
- The amount of drink consumed
- The sex of the individual
- The amount of food consumed
- The state of the human liver

Body Weight

The heavier the body the more drink it takes to achieve drunkenness.

The Amount of Drink Consumed

The amount of drink consumed and the strength of the alcohol in that drink relates to the state of drunkenness

The Sex of the Individual

Females will become intoxicated much faster than males. Compared to men, their body weight, water content and metabolism are all different.

The Amount of Food Consumed

The amount of food consumed both before and during the drinking session has an effect on drunkenness. Consumed food slows down the rate of alcohol entering the blood stream. But it is just a slow down. Nothing can be ingested that will speed up the elimination of alcohol from the blood stream.

The State of the Human Liver

It takes a healthy liver at least one hour to breakdown and eliminates the equivalent of a small glass of wine or one bottle of beer. (Health

Education Authority, UK. 1996) As a general rule, anyone who drinks more than either one bottle of wine or eight bottles of beer becomes a menace.

The faster a person drinks, and the more fizzy drink they use in their alcohol, the quicker they will become drunk. This is because they are drinking faster than their liver is capable of eliminating the alcohol from their body.

What makes all drunken people dangerous to handle is the fact that alcohol attacks and anaesthetizes the fore brain. This part of the brain is responsible for all aspects of learning, judgement and the regulation of behaviour (Scarf 1976 p. 87).

In reality this means that drunken people who are bereft of either humanity or compassion frequently confront you. They will have no moral or ethical guidelines in operation to prevent them from jumping all over your head when they feel like doing just that. It does not matter if they are from either high or low society, they will all kick just as hard.

You will be in even more danger if the customers using your venue are former convicts, thieves and trash rejected from every other drinking den in town. When these somewhat social cretins get drunk, your life is on the line if you screw up your risk assessment. There is no difference between the kicks of drunken dysfunctional people and psychopaths.

Neither group has any compassion or the ability to empathise with others. All their actions are motivated towards satisfying their own needs. The psychopath may use a certain amount of deviousness to manipulate others to achieve their objectives and the drunken person will just blunder on.

Visual Cues For Drunkenness

A high volume of drink consumption can induce the following types of observable behaviour:

- Slurred speech. The speech centres are located on the cortex. Alcohol directly affects the whole area of the cortex

- Inability to focus eyes

- Inability to stay awake because alcohol is a mental and physical depressant

- Stumbling gait/Poor balance/Inability to stand still. Alcohol affects the inner ear balance system and also delays the transmission of information between the brain and the legs

- Poor physical coordination and slow reaction times may render an individual incapable of sitting down in a chair or lighting a cigarette

- Slow response to any questions

  - Limited reasoning ability so that the drunken person feels they are in total command of their body. They feel superior to you, both physically and mentally
- Immunity to pain

  - Sudden mood swings/Amplified emotions

  - Verbal abuse

  - Paranoid to the extent that everything you say to the individual is misconstrued as an insult

  - Lowered inhibitions. More liable to argue, fight, urinate, defecate, cry etc. in public view

  - More frequent visits to the toilet. This is because consuming alcohol reduces the capacity of the kidneys to retain liquid

When to Caution the Drinker

For the floor supervisor there are two stages of drunkenness to watch out for that will demand your immediate intervention.

Stage 1-Caution

The early signs of drunkenness include: chanting, singing, over-friendly, slowed reflexes and clumsiness, possibly even while the drinker feels OK (hence the danger of drinking and then driving). If the person responds to your first two cautions to behave, then all is well.

Stage 2-Escort Off the Venue

The point when you need to say 'enough' is well before the person is displaying: swaying (even falling), severe slurring and mood swings - over-friendliness, anger or even sleepiness, a raised voice, belligerence, any behaviour that risks inconveniencing or endangers other customers, damages property and endangers the drunken person.
This stage demands a judgement call from the door supervisor. That will only come from personal experience and witnessing other door staff in action.

Asking a Drunken Person to Leave the Venue

Approaching a drunken person to eject them is a bad idea. First of all, try to identify the drunken person's friends and speak to them first. For example, say to them "Look man, your friend has had too much to drink, give him ten minutes and he will be falling all over the place. Another thing, the taxi cabs will not take him if he is too drunk, can you help?"
If you go directly to the drunken person and man handle him at all, you will run into grief from his friends. Always pre-empt this by appealing directly to them. This will prove to be a less confrontational and more productive approach.
When you are dealing with a solitary drunken person you must expect everything to happen in slow time. As you approach them, be calm, firm and initially, non-threatening.
Start by talking and keep talking, repeating the same simple request until it sinks in. Try to get the drunken person moving without touching them at all. Always expect 'drunks' to display at least six different forms of emotion before they reach the exit and you will not be surprised.
When the drunken person turns violent, there are two main factors to your advantage:

- Drunken people believe they are capable but their state renders them incapable

- Drunken people have no coordination or balance

There are three main factors that make drunken people dangerous:

- They are impervious to pain
- They have no conscience or humanity
- They will display sudden mood swings

To reiterate, there are many long-term effects of alcohol abuse to be taken into consideration before you physically interact with drunken people. These include:

- Social and psychological problems
- Damage to the liver, mouth, heart, stomach and brain.
- High blood pressure
- Poor hygiene

Because of these debilitating factors, you must refrain from neck restraints that may induce death, headshots that may exacerbate the brain damage and finally, body shots that may destroy the last vestiges in operating ability of the internal organs.

Walking Drunken Customers to The Door

When a drunken customer is walking in the vicinity of the exit use it as a golden opportunity to keep them moving out the door. If they are talking at a normal cadence and pitch (for a drunken customer), never interrupt. Keep them moving and talking with a good chat line of your own. Always try to maintain their friendly disposition. They will interpret any form of interdiction on your part as a threat.
Never try to practice a restraint on a compliant drunken person. Their reaction can be explosive. Remember that drunken people are impervious to pain and the alcohol has anaesthetized their reasoning ability. A restraint on a compliant drunken person will result in panic, fear and anger induced violence.

Using the Good Guy - Bad Guy Routine

You spot a solitary drunken customer who is making a pest of themselves at the bar area. If they remain in the bar their behaviour will become unpredictable in the anti-social direction. They will:

- Want to sleep

- Fall over and hurt themselves, others or else cause damage

- Start exaggerated and uninhibited emotional displays that include rapid mood swings from happy to raging

- Verbally abuse or fight with anyone who approaches them

The drunken person appears to have no friends that you can appeal to in the first instance. Your first task is to try and establish the individual's name from any source. After that, be prepared to constantly repeat a simple command that will get the drunken person off the premises. It will take at least two door supervisors to move a drunken customer to the door, the Leading Door Supervisor and his Back Up. The conversation and routine will go something like this...
The Leading Door Supervisor: First approach the drunken person and start to draw their attention. Try talking at first and then use a light touch to their forearm. 'Hello sir, it's time to go, come on, let's go home.'

Drunken person: ' Who the f*** are you? Piss off.'

The Leading Door Supervisor: 'Come on sir, time to go home, come on with me now.'

Drunken person: 'F*** off'

Note, at this stage, The Back Up is now standing close to and slightly behind the drunken person. Always stand as close as necessary to draw the drunk's attention to the numerical strength of the opposition who are about to separate him from his supply of electric soup.
The Leading Door Supervisor: 'Come along sir, time to go...No let him be. Don't touch him, he's OK. You're OK sir, come on now.'

Note that the Leading Door Supervisor is drawing the drunken person's attention to the bad guy who is breathing down his neck. The Leading

Door Supervisor is offering the drunken person the chance to go home in one piece. This routine may have to be repeated several times with accompanying hand gestures from the front to emphasize the presence of others.

An impasse will finally be reached when the drunken person fails to respond to the requests.

The Leading Door Supervisor throws up his hands in despair: 'I've tried everything, he will not come out, and I've tried everything'

The Back Up: 'OK, get an arm each and walk him out'

At this stage, the drunken person is walked out with a door supervisor on each arm, ready to respond to any physical resistance. This routine has three clear aims.

1. It focuses you on getting a drunken person off the premises with the minimum amount of force

2. All the customers see you using the minimum amount of force. They are potential witnesses for, and perhaps, against you

3. The bar maintains its 'Feel Good Factor'

The Violent Drunken Customer

There is one other type of reptile who will extend your patience and good nature to the limits. These are the drunken individuals who realise you are operating a minimum force policy, that is, you have not hit the bums, as yet, despite their drunken tirade. Once you get them to the door without a fight, they can shift their emotions from happy drunk to psycho reptile faster than you can close the door on their back. Usually they will vent their spleen on inanimate objects, rather than you, if you keep the door closed.

The following real life situation illustrates this. The drunken customer vacillated between drunken aggression, Reptile Mode and adrenalin highs for approximately ten minutes.

I observed my partner physically ejecting a drunken person from the venue, after failing to talk him out. At the door I took over the incident, allowing my partner to back off from this hostile scene. This procedure normally has the effect of de-escalating the situation. Not in this case, Mr. Anus became more agitated and frustrated despite all my attempts.

He then proceeded to rip up the bedding plants from the bar garden and throw them at me. That was just for openers, he then came close enough to spit on me and despite the admonishments of his friends he then proceeded to kick out. At this stage I closed the door on Mr. Anus, hoping he would cool down and depart with his friends. This ploy also failed.

Mr. Anus made his way to the side door and despite being restrained by his friend, he spat at, kicked and then tried to head butt me. At this stage, (Oh, Happy Days) he broke away from his friends so I pinned him to the wall with my version of the Vulcan Death Grip. I was amused to note that this move usually had my training partners grovelling, speechless and tapping out. I was now quite happily using twice as much force, but Mr. Anus was only whining, "Let me go, big man!" At least the hold stopped the kicking, spitting and head butting.

It was quite obvious that an adrenalin dump had taken place and the minimum force pressure point attack did not totally work. I also used this time out to ask Mr. Anus to desist from his physical abuse. Again, his friend intervened and walked him away from the door where he proceeded to kick out the garden lighting system.

Oh no, it's not over yet. Mr. Anus and friends parted company at this stage, he was now becoming too much of a liability. Mr. Anus was still in full Reptile Mode and collected half a house brick from a nearby building site and stuffed it into his back pocket. He then knocked on the front door, expecting the Man in Black to greet him. Thank goodness for CCTV and the bar monitor.

We waited for the arrival of the police, whereupon Mr. Anus dropped the half brick, smiled and then winked at me like we were lifelong buddies. It didn't work. When the police came back two hours later to take my statement on his alleged, and video taped, criminal damage and assault, Mr. Anus was still maintaining he was known as Elvis, The King.

Bibliography

Personal Communications, Corrections and Additions

Lowe, Chris (2009)

Mulholland, Graham (2009)

Ross, Ben (2008)

Books

Ardly R. (1970) *The Social Contract*. Atheneum. London

Bacon Seldon D. (1970) *Meeting the Problem of Alcoholism in the United States*. In Witney, Elizabeth D (ed) *World Dialogue on Alcohol and Drug Dependence*. Beacon Press, Boston, pp134-145.

Baron R.A. (1977) *Human Aggression*. Plenum Press. New York

Brewer M.B., & Crano W. D. (1994) *Social Psychology*. West Publishing Company. New York

Eysenck H & M. (1994) *Mind Watching*. MMB. London

Frijda N.H. (1989) *The Emotions*. Cambridge University Press. New York London

Greenfield S. (1997) *The Human Brain: A Guided Tour*. Weidenfeld & Nicolson. London

Hunt M. (1982) *The Universe Within*. Transworld Publishers Ltd. London

Kalat J.W. (1992) *Biological Psychology*. Brooks/Cole Publishing Company. Pacific Grove California

Koestler A. (1967) *The Ghost in the Machine*. Hutchinson. London

Le Bon, G. [1895] (1903) *The Crowd: A Study of the Popular Mind.* T.Fisher Unwin. London

MacLean P.D. (1973) *A Triune of the Brain and Behaviour.* University of Toronto Press. Toronto

MacLean, P.D. (1990) *The Triune Brain in Evolution: Role in Paleocerebral Functions.* Plenum Press, New York and London

Montagu A. (1975) *The Nature of Human Aggression.* OUP. London

Ornstein R. & Carstensen L. (1991) *Psychology-The Study of Human Experience.* Harcourt-Brace-Jovanovich. New York London

Rathus S.A., (1990) *Psychology,* Holt, Rinehart and Winston. London

Reber A.S. (1985) *The Penguin Dictionary of Psychology.* Penguin. London

Richardson F.M. (1978) *Fighting Spirit - A Study of Psychological Factors in War.* Leo Cooper. London

Rosenhan D.L. & Seligman M.E.P. (1995) *Abnormal Psychology.* W.W. Norton & Co. New York London

Rubington E. (1962) *'Failure' as a heavy drinker: The case of the chronic drunkenness offender on Skid Row.* In D.J. Pittman & C.R. Snyder (Eds.) *Society, Culture and Drinking Patterns.* John Wiley. New York

Scarf M. (1976) *Body Mind Behaviour.* Laurel Edition. New York

Spradley J.P. (1970) *You Owe Yourself a Drunk: An Ethnography of Urban Nomads.* Little Brown & Co. Boston

World Wide Web

(BCRCP, Community Counseling & Crisis Center, 2001) Butler County Rape Crisis Program. *Drug Facilitated Rape.* http://www.helpandhealing.org

National Institute of Occupational Safety and Health (USA, 1995). http://www.cdc.gov/niosh/homicide.html

(WAVAW, 2001-2) http://www.wavaw.ca/start.htm

Go to http://www.google.com Type in 'Anatomy of a Choke'. This will take you to the two sites for the International Judo Federation for an informative article called 'The Anatomy of a Choke'.

(WRCC, 2003) Women's Rape Crisis Center. *Date Rape Drugs* http://www.stoprapevermont.org/wrcc.html

Documents

Focus on Alcohol - *A Guide to Drinking and Health* (2002) Health Promotion Agency (NI)

Studies

Argyle, M., et al. (1970) *The Communication of Inferior and Superior Attitudes by Verbal and Non-verbal Signals*, British Journal of Social and Clinical Psychology, Vol. 9, part 3, September, pp. 222-231.

Frank, M. G. & Gilovich, T. (1988) *The dark side of self and social perception: Black uniforms and aggression in professional sports*. Journal of Personality and Social Psychology. 54, pp74-85.

Leather, P. & Lawrence, C. (1995) *Perceiving pub violence: The symbolic influence of social and environmental factors*. British Journal of Social Psychology. 34, pp 395-407.

Mehrabian, Albert, and Wiener, Morton. (1967) *Decoding of Inconsistent Communications*. Journal of Personality and Social Psychology, Vol. 6, No. 1, May, pp109-114

Oestreich, Herb. (1999) *Let's Dump the 55%, 38%, 7% Rule*, Transitions, (National Transit Institute), Vol. 7, No. 2

Thomas-Kilmann Conflict Mode Instrument, (1974) Tuxedo NY: Xicom

Magazines

Berkowitz, L (September, 1968) *Impulse, aggression and the gun.* Psychology Today pp18-22.

Watch out for the next volume in this series:

The Door Supervisor: The Physical Skills

Chapters include:

The Use of Force Model
Medical Effects of Physical Intervention
Physical Intervention
Restraints
Pressure Points
Situational Drills
Bar Fights
Street Fighting
Training Notes